Advance Praise

A Principal's Notebook

A Principal's Notebook is a warm and stirring history of a truly democratic public school in which the concept of the "caring community" was embodied in every aspect of a student's learning—and, perhaps even more important, in the way the voices and decisions of young people helped to shape its governance. Dave Lehman is one of those inspiring.but unassuming leaders who placed democracy and equity and the willingness to listen to young people at the very center of his life's vocation. In the present decade, when the watchwords of too many schools and districts are "compliance" and "control," thousands of good teachers will be grateful to Dave Lehman for holding up a wiser vision of the kind of education every child deserves.

—Jonathan Kozol
National Book Award winner

Dave Lehman has always walked the walk, not just talking about school leadership and innovation, but demonstrating what is possible at his school. His counsel and judgment has informed the work of hundreds of educators, myself included. And now that work can spread further through this volume of practice-informed wisdom. What he offers in *A Principal's Notebook* is a handbook for any school leader, teacher, parent, or aspiring educator as they work to build schools of meaning and engagement for our children and communities. I will be a better leader because finally Dave has shared his life captured in the famous Lehman notebooks.

—George Wood
Superintendent, Federal Hocking Local Schools

Advance Praise (Continued)

Everything Dave Lehman writes in *A Principal's Notebook* brings back cherished memories. He offers everyday wisdom and advice to cut through the complexity of operating a school as a democracy, while sharing the joys and compromises made over 30 years of leading a pioneering public school. I'm ready to start again with this book in hand!
—Deborah Meier
Acclaimed school founder, author, and former Senior Scholar, Steinhardt School of Education, New York University

In A Principal's Notebook, Dave Lehman writes with passion, humility, and detail as to how his remarkable secondary school has sustained itself over the course of time. Lehman provides educators of today with a rare gift, his experiences in cultivating an educative community that provides an education for youth that equips them in the remaking of a robust democratic society for all. This book couldn't be more timely.
—Carl Glickman
Professor Emeritus, the University of Georgia and author, *Renewing America's Schools* and *Revolutionizing America's Schools*

This book is a real world example of how intentionally building trusting relationships between student peers and students and their teachers can promote real learning. After reading *A Principal's Notebook*, my hope is that you will be able to include at least some of the successful practices from LACS, so that your students benefit from them as well.
—Michele Mattoon
Director, National School Reform Faculty (NSRF)

David gives the reader an incredible perspective on education reform today. Decades ago he was doing what some people are still talking about today. This book can be used as a bible for anyone starting a school today. The details will help anyone doing day to day as well as helping others see the struggle it takes to create a great school. After reading *A Principal's Notebook*, you will be amazed that 50 years later most schools aren't yet doing the things David did. The book offers hope and more. It offers a template for how others could do a student democratic school.

—Dennis Littky
Co-Founder, Big Picture Learning, The Met School, and College Unbound

Education is about relationships. This is the heart of Dave Lehman's *A Principal's Notebook*. This book gives readers both a history of how Lehman Alternative Community School was born, as well as the guiding principles, practices, and institutional structures that made it so successful. People need a structure that prioritizes, develops, and models healthy, caring relationships in order to realistically learn how to relate in a caring, cooperative, and educational manner. This book provides not only a guide and model for developing good schools but for developing a healthy and democratic nation.

—Ira Rabois
Educator and Author, *Compassionate Critical Thinking: How Mindfulness, Creativity, Empathy and Socratic Questioning Can Transform Teaching.*

A Principal's Notebook

A Principal's Notebook

Lessons for Today from a Pioneering Public School

Dave Lehman

A Principal's Notebook
Lessons for Today from a Pioneering Public School

Alternative Education Resource Organization
417 Roslyn Road
Roslyn Heights, NY 11577

Cover: Black Dog Designs
Layout: Isaac Graves

Printed in the United States of America.

Library of Congress Control Number: 2018935057
ISBN: 978-0986016028

To all the past and present staff of the Lehman Alternative Community School. You are, and have been from the beginning, the backbone—indeed the very heart—of our school. You have been family, giving me confidence, honest feedback, support and care, sharing and celebrating successes while persevering through the hardships, setback, and losses. Each of you could tell your own story, different, yet cut from the same cloth. To all of you I say "Thank You!"

Contents

Foreword

At the outset the reader might simply ask: why did you write such a book? I would reply that hopefully the chapters that follow will provide: 1) educators both with a detailed description of the key elements of what subsequently became the "Lehman[1] Alternative Community School," and 2) inspiration for current educators to continue developing innovative, student-centered, community-based, neo-progressive secondary schools. At the beginning of each chapter I have given a brief personal story related to the topic of that chapter. And after each chapter I have provided possible discussion questions that might be of use to those starting their own alternative school. A list of resources is included which may also be of help. But first, what's the back-story? How did I get involved in education—particularly "alternative education"— in the first place?

*****

1. The discerning reader will note the word "Lehman" in the name of the school is the same as the last name of the author. In 2004, upon my retirement as principal of the Alternative Community School—a public alternative secondary school, grades six through twelve—I attended the annual end-of-year gathering for all the district administrators of the Ithaca City School District in the state of New York, hosted by the superintendent and her husband. Midway through the evening, the superintendent asked my wife, Judy, and I to sit down and face a group of 30 administrators lined up in front of us. Each of them was holding a blank square of poster board and on the superintendent's signal they all turned these around. It spelled "Lehman Alternative Community School." Needless to say Judy and I were totally surprised! The superintendent then quickly explained that, at her request, the school board had agreed to rename the school building after us. Subsequently it was approved by the full student body that the school would be named the Lehman Alternative Community School.

In the winter of 1957 I was a high school junior at George Washington High School in Alexandria, Virginia. During basketball practice, we were working on our pressing defense during which you guard your opponent extra closely, trying to intercept a pass or take the ball away. Suddenly I was struck in my cheekbone, just below my left eye. Wham! I went down and out, briefly knocked unconscious by the head fake of the teammate I was guarding. The Coach had me sit down, and although I had recovered consciousness, I had a terrible headache and couldn't see clearly out of my left eye, so he told me to shower and get dressed. I did so, but rather than wait and catch the city bus, I found a dime in my pocket and used the pay phone in the lobby of the front hall to call my parents to come pick me up, which my dad did, wondering what had happened.

It turned out I had a compound fracture of the left cheekbone and internal hemorrhaging behind my left eye. It hurt like hell, and I was dizzy and faint with blurry vision in that left eye. For several weeks I spent time largely in bed with the shades drawn as any light hurt my eyes and made the headache worse. Thanks to my parents, particularly my mother—who was home and not teaching kindergarten at the time—I fully recovered in about two months and was finally able to return to high school, but the basketball season was over for me—too risky, the doctor said.

The one thing I remember most vividly was yearning to see and talk with my friends; guys from the basketball team, guys from the dance/rock band I played in, and others. I realized that school was really about relationships! That's why I wanted to get better, to get back to school and to see those guys! It wasn't the classes I missed, and not even so much playing basketball again—I was even forbidden by the doctor to play baseball later that spring for fear I might have another concussion since my whole head, brain, and eyes were still healing and too vulnerable to take the risk—I missed those relationships.

*****

So what was it that led me to become a teacher? A principal? An educator? One might say I was influenced early in my life by my mother who was a kindergarten teacher—maybe even my grandmother who wrote children's books—or my older brother who graduated from college when I graduated from high school, since he started teaching high school math and coaching sports. But it wasn't evident at that time because I went to Ohio Wesleyan University as a pre-veterinary student. As a kid I always had a pet dog (our little beagle, Patches, slept on the lounge chair in my bedroom throughout my recovery from the broken cheekbone concussion!), and for several years I worked as a stable-boy at a horseback riding school, and loved to ride and be around the horses.

No, it was in one of those morning chapel programs that we were required to attend every Monday, Wednesday, and Friday at Ohio Wesleyan University. The speaker was former Olympic athlete Bobby Jones. He talked about choosing to do something with your life to help others, to make a difference, and for some reason it hit home hard with me. I left the auditorium emotionally drained. I went to the little chapel across the street from the main campus and actually cried. I was so excited, so over-joyed. Quite simply, I had decided what I really wanted to do with my life: work with young people. It was that experience, and my earlier feeling about relationships, that subtly shaped my decision to become a high school biology teacher, a basketball and baseball coach, and to work with young people through church groups and summer camps. Thus, I majored in Religion with an emphasis on Religious

Education, completed minors in Botany and Zoology, and took the required education courses to be certified as a teacher.

There were five other experiences which had a profound effect on me in forming the background for my becoming principal, first of a junior high school, and then, as it expanded, a middle-high school, grades six through twelve. The first experience was also in high school, the second came during my first year of teaching high school biology at Homewood-Flossmoor High School in Illinois, the third while a graduate student at the University of Virginia where I attended on a National Science Foundation fellowship, the fourth when I was completing my PhD at the University of Texas in Austin and had the opportunity to leave for a year to direct a biology teaching project for UNESCO in Ghana, West Africa, and the fifth was the creation of a "free school" grades K-12 called Greenbriar, outside of Austin, Texas.

The other profound high school experience also was an outgrowth of my basketball playing when in my senior year. From the window at the end of the third floor hallway where my locker was located, one could see across the raised bed of railroad tracks to Parker Gray High School, the "Negro" high school in Alexandria. The Parker Gray players, like my teammates at GWHS and myself, were one of the top high school basketball teams in the state of Virginia. Both our teams went to the state championships my junior and senior years. Because our high schools were segregated, we did not, and could not, play Parker Gray. I, and many of my teammates, thought that was ludicrous and kept asking our coach if we could at least play them in a scrimmage game. Finally, our respective school administrations agreed to allow us to attend one of their games, and for them to attend one of ours. That seemed so lame that my good friends and one of my teammates and I would go on Saturdays to various local playgrounds where a number of Parker Gray players played, and join them in some great pick-up basketball! This had a major impact on my beginning to question such blatant racism, and the role of schools.

After graduating from high school I became a high school biology teacher and assistant basketball coach at Homewood-Flossmoor High School, located in a suburb southwest of Chicago. It was here that I discovered there was another way to teach science, specifically biology, with an inquiry, heavily laboratory focused approach. By the end of that first year of teaching biology, using a standard, albeit outdated, textbook, I had almost daily migraine headaches and knew that something had to change. Fortunately, I discovered the "experimental edition" of the Biological Sciences Curriculum Study, or BSCS, specifically the "blue version," which was for me an exciting molecular approach to teaching high school biology. My vice principal supported me in ordering the paperback experimental editions of the laboratory/field-studies/text, and allowed me to completely redesign and equip two of the biology classrooms as genuine laboratories. The essential difference for me as a teacher was that I no longer had to know—or pretend to know—literally everything about biology. I could respond to student questions with, "I don't know; let's look into that!" It also gave students a chance to discover things on their own, to question things, and to work collaboratively with each other and with me in a new way as their teacher/mentor/facilitator.

The above experience led me to apply for, and receive, a National Science Fellowship to attend the University of Virginia to study the BSCS approach to teaching high school biology. This was a one year intensive graduate school study (including a summer on an Association of Southeastern Biologists scholarship to study Ecology at the UVA Mountain Lake Biological Research Station) offering an opportunity to become re-excited by such courses as "Molecular Genetics," "Comparative Endocrinology," and "Neurobiology." But it was my experience with my fellow graduate students that again convinced me of the need to address the blatant racism in 1964-65 as evidenced at the University and in the town of Charlottesville. There were four African American biology teachers in my program and I used to study with them—something the other white biology teachers did not do! And it was in a local bar where the five of us went for a beer one evening, that despite the Civil Rights Act, we sat for a half-hour waiting to be served, and never were, while several whites came after us and were served. It also was in Charlottesville that we joined a student protest march in support of the University's African American cafeteria workers who were being discriminated against in their pay and working conditions.

After completing my Masters in Education at UVA, I decided to go for a PhD— believing that perhaps I could make an even greater impact in education by becoming a science education professor. I was accepted to a program in science education at the University of Texas in Austin. In my next to last year of doctoral studies, I was working as a Project Associate for BSCS, running a laboratory in the University's Science Education Center, doing trial runs of laboratory exercises in the experimental editions of their high school Laboratory Block program. My secretary took a call from UNESCO (United Nations Educational, Scientific, and Cultural Organization). The caller was asking for someone from our center to be the laboratory/field studies consultant to join the "UNESCO Pilot Project for Teaching Biology in English Speaking African Secondary Schools." I said I would check and someone would get back to them, and I hung up. Our director was unavailable, as well as the other graduate students in the department, so I called back to say, "Yes, I'm interested and available!" This led to my full year appointment as laboratory/field studies consultant of the "Biology Pilot Project" housed at the University College of Cape Coast, outside Cape Coast, Ghana in West Africa.

Upon arriving at the University College of Cape Coast I was given a bungalow for my family and myself with a cook and our own car and driver. We then met as a whole group in one of the lecture halls in the science building and heard from the two co-directors of their plans for the Project. One was an invertebrate zoology professor from the University of Pittsburgh and the other a British ex-patriot from the University of Sierra Leone in Freetown. They told their "plan" to the gathered members of the Project. There were 17 "Consultants" from 9 different countries, and 17 "Participants" from 14 English-speaking African nations,[2] most of them from prestigious positions such as Director of Science Education for their African nation. The co-directors' plan was that they themselves would write a new textbook for the English-speaking African secondary schools, inviting the African "Participants" to comment on various chapters as they were being written. Also, the "Participants," were housed in the college student dormitories with one shared bathroom on each floor, while the "Consultants" were housed in bungalows like myself. We "Consultants" also were given commissary privileges (primarily liquor at really low prices) at the UN Embassy in the Capital, Accra. Needless to say the Africans were out-raged by their second-class treatment, and refused to come to the next session! Subsequently, the Director of Science Education at UNESCO, who was attending to kick-off the Project, came to me to say the professor from the University of Pittsburgh was not feeling well and was going to have to return to the States, while the professor from Sierra Leone, was going to have to return to Freetown as he was only able to attend the Project second semester: would I direct the Project?

Not wanting to give up the whole thing at this point, I said I would, but only given certain conditions: 1) all the Participants would immediately be housed temporarily in

2. The African writers were from Somalia, Nigeria, Ghana, Liberia, Botswana, UAR (Egypt), Kenya, Tanzania, Ethiopia, Lesotho, Malawi, Uganda, Zambia, and the Sudan. The UNESCO consultants were from the United States, England, Czechoslovakia, Sweden USSR (Russia), and these African Countries: Sierra Leone, Ghana, Uganda, and the Sudan.

a motel a few miles from campus with meals prepared in the interim by kitchen staff in a university guest house, 2) the Participants subsequently would be called the "Writers" and would be housed in three bungalows with cooks, vans, and drivers, 3) the commissary privileges would be shared equally by Writers and Consultants, 4) we would no longer meet in the lecture hall, but would meet around a conference table in a room in the science faculty of the College, and 5) that we would begin again asking the Writers what they would like to do. All of this was agreed to, and done, and we collectively decided to produce a text, with laboratory and field activities integrated throughout a series of 12 chapters, to be titled "Investigating Living Things: Introductory Biology for Secondary Schools," with an accompanying Teachers' Guide, a "Handbook for Microbiology" (our microbiologist was from Russia), and we also created a series of 8mm film loops with Teachers' Guides (we had a Czechoslovakian film director and a Ghanaian cameraman). Fortunately all these goals were met collaboratively, and everyone went home in July with a box of film loops, and fully illustrated paperback books with Teachers Guides (we had a British artist), and these were actually printed in the print shop of the University College of Cape Coast!

This was without a doubt the most powerful learning experience of my life. I learned so much about Africa, human relations, and leadership. I vowed upon returning to complete my PhD not with the intention to seek a professorship in science education, but to help bring change to education as I'd known it. Subsequently, I joined with a small group of educators and counter-culture young adults in Austin to found a K-12, democratically-run, "free school," where students could learn what they wanted, with much opportunity for creativity, play, art, and music. I was the nominal "Principal" and taught such things as "Collecting and Eating Wild Foods," "A History of West Africa," "Wood-carving," and whatever else interested students. After two and a half years, I became convinced that much of what I had learned being part of the "free school" should be available to young people in public schools. After a one year stint as the Children's Minister at the non-denominational, progressive First Community Church in Upper Arlington, outside Columbus, Ohio (they ostensibly were to develop a progressive pre-K through high school, but never followed through). I left to join the New Schools Exchange collective, located on a small organic farm and garden—Shanti Gardens—not far from Columbus.

This all, then, forms the backdrop of experiences that subsequently led me to Ithaca, New York and the "New Junior High Program." I felt I was ready for a radical adventure into alternative public secondary education!

But first, a word about the book's title, *A Principal's Notebook*. For those who were a part of NJHP or ACHS or ACS, they will remember my leather-bound notebook. Although it began as a more conventional black bound loose-leaf notebook, I found a leather-bound, three-quarter sized, loose-leaf, 3-ring notebook—which I still use!—and have patched the cover at least a couple of times. During those years of principal-ing and teaching at what was to become LACS, I used that notebook for everything. There was a center section with a 2-weeks-at-a-glance calendar format that I drew-up each school year; a section for notes of all the kinds of meetings that happened every week—district-wide administrators' meetings, weekly school staff meetings, conferences with individual or small groups of staff, students, and/or parents/caregivers—as well as notes from various alternative education conferences I attended, a section to write down names of books and articles I wanted to remember to read, and people to contact. I carried this with me everywhere, and it is from *The Notebook* that I have taken much for this book.

Lastly, where did my personal/professional "title"—"Dr. Dave"—come from? The first thing you would probably think is that it is simply a reference to the fact that I have a PhD, thus the "Dr." But the actual source of this didn't come until several years into my principal-ship. As you've already learned, I was an athlete throughout high school and college, playing not only basketball, but baseball as well (at OWU I was the captain my senior year, and the third baseman of the Ohio Conference all star team that year, ending my four year college career with a life-time batting average of .385). It was basketball in particular that I loved to play with our students and staff, and it was one of the students who began calling me the tag, "Dr. Dave," channeling the pro basketball player, Julius Erving— "Dr. J"—known for his outstanding jump-shot. Mine was not quite that good, but I did have a pretty decent shot for an old fella. Although few knew that history, for whatever reason it stuck: I had become "Dr. Dave."

The book is organized into five chapters, as well as this "Foreword," an "Afterword," and an "Appendix." It begins with the New Junior High Program and ends with the various ways in which student learning is evaluated. With each chapter I have provided some possible "Discussion Questions," particularly for those planning to start a democratically-run alternative school, and some additional "Resources" which may be helpful.

Chapter One

In the Beginning
The New Junior High Program

I was on the way to school one morning that first year of the New Junior High Program (NJHP) when I spotted a dead raccoon on the roadside. It looked to be a fresh road-kill, and because one of the three courses I was teaching at the time was "Comparative Dissection," I picked-up the critter and put "it" (wasn't clear to me at the time if it was a male or female) in the car. Come class time, I retrieved my specimen for dissection. The seventh and eighth graders and I were excited, if somewhat apprehensive (none of my college zoology classes had involved dissecting a raccoon, but I thought, "how hard can it be?"). As with the fish and frogs we had already dissected, it seemed logical to turn the raccoon on his back (it had become obvious that it was a male) and with a scalpel and scissors, make an incision in the midline of the underside, or belly of the animal. Thus, I spread him out on the dissecting tray—appropriately pinning-down his four legs with dissecting needles and pins—and opened the abdomen. Immediately an extremely offensive odor arose from the carcass causing me quickly to open the window in our make-shift science lab, send a student to retrieve an electric fan from an adjacent room, and alert those in the rooms nearest ours to open all of their windows to try and get as much cross ventilation as possible to blow through the second floor of our building! Soon thereafter, most of the teachers and students evacuated the building—beating all previous fire drill departure times—while

I quickly closed up our "demonstration," wrapped it in newspaper, and discarded it in a trash can outside in the rear of the building!

Fast-forward the film a few years: we were in the E-building wing of Ithaca High School [see the next chapter]. There's that old saying, "Twice burned, once learned!" Our science teacher [with increased enrollment allowing the hire of a part-time science teacher, I now only taught one course] was an occasional deer hunter and thought it would be a great experience for his students actually to put together a deer skeleton. Thus, he completely gutted and skinned-out a deer he'd recently killed and brought the bones in a large garbage bag to school. There still was a considerable portion of muscle, tendons, and ligaments that needed to be cleaned, and his thought was—let the "elements" clean the rest of the carcass. So, we put the "un-cleaned" bones on a couple of trays ["borrowed" from the IHS cafeteria!] on the roof of E-building [there was a ladder to the roof of the one-story building going out of my office; formerly the head custodian's office], and proceeded to forget about it, believing the weather and various carrion feeders would, in time, clean the bones. It was not many weeks before we, and the IHS staff began to notice a rather pungent odor coming from E-building! [Of course it was no surprise to the high school staff that there should be a disagreeable odor coming from "The Alternate," as our school was referred to; after all, we did get some of their building space!] Remembering the deer skeleton on the roof, that day, waiting until well after school, the science teacher and I scaled the ladder, placed the deer skeleton—still not completely "cleaned"—into a garbage bag, and placed it in the trunk of his car for him to take home. The high school custodians and principal commented the next day that the odor seemed to have mysteriously disappeared—and I simply acknowledged that; indeed, it did seem to have disappeared. Needless to say, in all my future years as principal and science teacher, we never again dealt with any animal skeletons!

*****

I was initially hired as a 0.6 science/health teacher and 0.4 administrator/principal, and began that first school year, in 1974, the April before we opened in September, spending much of those first few spring and summer months operating out of borrowed office space in the Ithaca City School District administrative office building. In retrospect, not such a bad idea as it provided virtually daily contact with the district administrators—superintendent, assistant superintendent for secondary schools, district business manager, and particularly some wonderful secretarial office staff—as well as valuable access to their central photocopying machines! That first summer I also commuted to the State University of New York (SUNY) at Cortland to take additional required courses to complete my New York State administrators certificate [despite the fact that I had graduate degrees in science education—a PhD in curriculum and development from the University of Texas at Austin, and an MEd from The University of Virginia— as well as a BA in religion from Ohio Wesleyan University with minors in botany and zoology, and certification as a biology teacher]. As the "Teacher/Administrator," even though as a 0.4 administrator, I technically was not eligible to be a member of the "Principals' Association," I was allowed to attend their meetings. Our New Junior High Program "Lavender Proposal," written by a blue-ribbon district committee, spelled-out in detail just how this new alternative junior high was to be organized, including that we were to have mini-courses taught every five weeks with new offerings generated for each new 5-week period. By the end of the fourth or fifth 5-week cycles, the staff and students agreed to go to 7-week cycles; the 5-week time periods were just too short and left little time to prepare new courses. Between each of these cycles we also inserted a day to give staff a chance to work on the new mini-courses while students did various community service activities including helping to shelve books at the Tompkins County Library, assisting in classes at Central Elementary School, tutoring special education students, and assisting with senior citizens in local retirement homes. Besides teaching the "Comparative Dissection" mini-course mentioned in the Foreword, I taught everything from a ninth-grade "Earth Science" course, "CB Radios" (one of our student's dad was a trucker and had a real CB radio!—we made little AM radios in class), "Super 8mm Film Making," "Local Animals and Plants," to "Human Nutrition," "Human Sexuality," "Beginning First Aid," and "Alternative Energy."

The teaching staff allocation was based on the Ithaca Teachers Association contracted student/teacher ratio. For each 18.65 students in the secondary schools, 1.0 teacher equivalents (certified secondary school teachers or the rough equivalent of two para-professionals) could be hired; the initial staff thus included:

- 0.7 math teacher
- 0.7 shared by two part-time English teachers
- 0.7 social studies teacher
- Full-time Spanish teacher/guidance counselor (French and German also were provided by a retired teacher, and Latin by a volunteer professor from Ithaca College)
- Full-time art/music teacher
- 0.3 PE teacher who also had a part-time after-school position across the street at a local neighborhood center, the Greater Ithaca Activities Center (GIAC)
- 0.6 custodian, and school district bus driver, who also taught photography and ran our dark room
- 0.6 clerk/secretary
- Part-time nurse*

- Part-time social worker*
- Part-time school psychologist*

[*These three support personnel had shared assignments, serving one day or a half-day each week at NJHP, and part-time in other schools in the district.]

The first year we had 65 students and thus we were eligible to hire 3.5 teaching staff, and were given an additional 0.5 to cover the assignment of one of our teachers as an "involuntary transfer" from one of the other middle schools. It's important to note here, that although we had a fixed staff allocation, we utilized volunteers from the community and used existing community programs for young people to expand and broaden our students' learning opportunities.

Staff met weekly in participatory democratic meetings to share successes, address issues and concerns (such as arranging room use and resolving scheduling conflicts), discuss student academic performance, decide on disciplinary actions, create student committees, plan all school events, address rumors in the community about the school, and prepare for each upcoming 5-week cycle of classes. This commitment to working democratically remains a cornerstone of staff relations, and was new for most staff members, requiring patience and a commitment of significant time to developing a healthy community among the staff, learning to conduct meetings in an egalitarian fashion.

Our "school house" for those first 65 students (in the typical grades 7, 8, and 9 for a junior high school) was a two-story, brick, former New York State Gas and Electric Company (NYSEG) office building[1], which more recently had been a school district office building. We were able to create ten "classrooms"—using that term loosely—a shared office space, a men's room downstairs and women's room upstairs (part of which also served as the nurse's station when she was there one day a week), and the infamous "lounge." Because students typically had one "free period" (no assigned classes) and no study halls in their schedules, the lounge was a place they could hangout between classes. They also could "sign-out" (and sign back in!) to go off campus, and some did so to go to lunch since downtown was just a few blocks away. Although occasionally there was unruly behavior in the lounge, or students sometimes were late returning from off campus, by and large these "privileges" were not abused.

Located on the corner of Court and Plain streets, we made use of an asphalt basketball court and small playing field on the east side. Our building was across the street from the back entrance to a local Catholic school and across another corner to "Jake's," a small grocery store/delicatessen run for many years by Jake and his wife. They were both survivors of Auschwitz, and became friends of the school, often speaking with students and staff about their memories of that horrendous experience. Kitty-corner down the street a half-block was the neighborhood center, the Greater Ithaca Activities Center (GIAC), at which our students were welcome to use their facilities. We worked hard to have positive relations with the center, and I served two terms as their Board President. It was attached to the back of Central Elementary School (where our students who were eligible for free and reduced lunch could go for lunch), and another two blocks down the street was the Tompkins County Library that was essentially our school library. Directly behind our building was the school District stockroom of various school supplies and the maintenance shop for the District's vehicles. I use the

1. The original location recommended in the "Lavender Proposal" was to have been the building known as the "Tin Can," the one-story Quonset hut and former Naval Reserve Center, which housed the Ithaca Youth Bureau, the pre-K Head Start program and some maintenance facilities of the school district.

past tense here because none of these buildings are still there. The block is now a large grassy vacant lot with a neighborhood swimming pool directly across from GIAC. Our beloved NJHP and the district buildings behind it were all torn down, and—unknown to us as it turned out—the underground, old fuel oil storage tanks were removed according to a special EPA-approved procedure, with the "contaminated" ground dug up and hauled away. This was all done many years after our school moved to the E-building wing of Ithaca High School, and then to the school's "permanent" location in the former West Hill Elementary School.

The overwhelming majority of the staff were new to what was being called "alternative education" throughout the country in the '60s and '70s, but were committed to doing school differently: making it student-centered and democratically run. The school day included six 50-minute periods at least three times per week (some met all five days), two periods for student "Committees" for everything from "School Maintenance" and "Beautification," to "Curriculum Planning" and "Review Board" (a student court). Two periods per week were also set aside for "Family Group" (FG—initially there were seven), known as "Advisory Groups" in some alternative schools, and even in some "conventional" middle schools. Family Groups were typically composed of 8-10 students meeting with a staff "Family Group Leader" who was responsible for the following "essential functions:"

- Take daily attendance for all FG members (later to be done by the 2nd period teacher)
- Advise FG students in planning their schedules for each academic "cycle"
- Keep track of how FG students are doing through reviewing staff evaluation reports on progress in their various courses and projects

- Communicate with parents/caregivers[2] through conferences and phone calls
- Share intra-school announcements and information with FG students
- Serve as first contact with behavior issues from other staff about their FG students
- Plan regular weekly activities with their FG students [See Chapter 4 for more about Family Groups.]

Each Monday afternoon there was the democratically-run "All School Meeting" (ASM), attended by all staff and students [see Chapter 3 for more about ASMs].

Students could also do weekly "apprenticeships" through the Learning Web, a project of the Center for Religion, Ethics and Social Policy (CRESP) at Cornell University, which placed students with a community mentor. Students met with their mentors to do such things as horse-shoeing (not playing horseshoes, but actually learning how to "shoe" horses!), weaving, cabinet making, motorcycle repair, conversational French, graphic design, big game conservation, short order cooking, carpentry, computer programming, child care, stereo repair, and horticulture. Learning Web opportunities also included weekly placements at local businesses, community agencies, and a popular local FM radio station, for all of which free community bus tickets enabled our students to access these more readily. Additionally, GIAC allowed us to use their woodshop and we in turn allowed them to use our photography-darkroom. Thus, our students had numerous weekly learning opportunities outside of our building throughout the community. And there was one other thing

2. We made this change to "parents/caregivers" as a result of the work of the "Families Against Racism" group of our students, staff, and parents during the summer of 1994 as we became aware of a number of our students who were not being raised by their biological parents, but by grandparents, other relatives, or adoptive families.

that happened outside of the building, just across Court Street, under a big old oak tree—the smokers. With only a couple of staff who were smokers, they volunteered to simply step off school grounds to take their cigarette breaks, and therefore that was where the student smokers could go, thus avoiding the strict district policy of no smoking on school grounds with the punishment being out-of-school suspension. We didn't exactly condone their smoking, just didn't want it to become such a big issue and cause students to miss school.

There was time each week for students also to participate in various learning activities throughout the greater Ithaca community, such as the special programs of the "Ithaca Youth Bureau"—bicycle repair, automotive maintenance, or a special metal shop program making high-quality hunting knives. One particularly popular program run by staff of the Youth Bureau was initially called "Outside the Four Walls," then later became known as "Nature and Survival," and included learning outdoor camping skills, canoeing, kayaking, back-packing, cross-country skiing, and participating in two several day trips in November and February.

Besides the Ithaca Youth Bureau and its various programs, and the Learning Web with their advocacy for young people in the community, there also was the "Interim Family" organization run out of the "Ithaca Family and Children's Center," and the "Group Homes of Tompkins County." Both of these agencies worked with young people who had family troubles, or were wards of the state, or were part of the juvenile justice system, and thus typically some of the students most desperately in need of an alternative school program[3]. Working closely with these organizations was essential in the early years of NJHP as these were many of the disenfranchised youth we were most anxious to serve. Additionally, already having made contact with GIAC (as well as Central Elementary School and subsequently "Southside," the other downtown neighborhood center), which was serving predominantly the African American youth of the downtown area, we had the opportunity to meet parents/caregivers who were seeking a better educational experience for their young people.

Probably the singular most effective way we built a real sense of democratic community those first three years was through the weeklong Spring Camping Trip. [For more about some memorable incidents on Camping Trips, see the Intro to Chapter 3.] We took everyone we could, staff and students, and even some parents/caregivers. We tent-camped in small groups we called "Basecamps," which included a staff "Basecamp Leader." This all began with everyone pitching-in to raise funds for the trip—from paying our school bus drivers to purchasing food and paying the camping fees—with raffle tickets being our main fund-raiser. These tickets were made by handset type and printed on the old printing press that we had brought from East Hill! It was in the Basecamp groups that not only funds were raised, but once at our campsite, meals were prepared and different daily activities were planned, from hiking and fishing to collecting fire wood and washing dishes. A surprising number of students each year not only had never been tent-camping and never prepared their own meals, but also had never even been away from home, never having taken a trip outside of Ithaca! Thus there was a huge amount to learn, particularly about how to share the work and do things together. Those who did have outdoor experience taught the others who did not have outdoor experience—and even many

3. In those first months of being on the job I made contact with these agencies and was subsequently invited to join the boards of the Youth Bureau, Interim Families, Group Homes, and GIAC, serving two terms as the president of the GIAC board, initiating with a planning group, the "Martin Luther King Jr. Community Breakfast" on Dr. King's birthday. At the end of the NJHP three-year trial period, when, due to district-wide declining enrollment in secondary schools, we were forced to lose our African-American PE teacher—"last hired, first fired"—after which I helped form and chaired the district's "Affirmative Action Committee," co-authoring the district's "Affirmative Action Plan."

of the staff who were not experienced campers—not only the essential survival skills, but also how to ditch your tent so your things didn't get soaked when it rained. In the second and third years this Spring Camping Trip also came to include a subgroup of cross-country biking students and staff, and another subgroup of canoeing students and staff who started a day or two earlier than the rest, and arrived at our campsite with much fanfare, a couple of days after the main group had set up camp. These adventures contributed valuable lessons in self-confidence, tolerance, problem solving, and were evidence that there are many different kinds of valuable skills.

We're often asked, "How did you get started? How did your alternative secondary school begin?" After serving as the NYSEG office building, our NJHP building initially had served several years in the early 1970s as the home of a junior high fore-runner to our school, named "Markles Flats" after an eccentric family that had lived in the downtown area of Ithaca known as "the Flats." This junior high program had been run as an outreach project by the college students in the Human Affairs Program (HAP) at Cornell University. There are numerous wild stories of all kinds, largely perpetuated by a couple of very outspoken women from an ultra fundamentalist group who often appeared on a local talk radio show. This, along with the first year's disappointing results of the Cornell HAP students efforts, followed by the resignation of the director of their project because of their failure to attract a sufficient number of students-of-color, led to the program being closed. It then re-opened with a new "principal" appointed by the School Board, only to be closed again, and an "Interim Program" temporarily re-located to a few classrooms in a wing of DeWitt Junior High School. Subsequently, the superintendent of schools, with school board approval, appointed a blue ribbon, 21 member "Advisory Committee on Alternate Education" to study and make recommendations regarding the need for "alternate education" in the Ithaca City School District. They presented their findings in August of 1973 in a report that began with the following powerful quote from none other than Thomas Jefferson:

> Freedom is the right to choose, the right to create for oneself the alternatives of choice. Without the possibility of choice, and the exercise of choice, a man is not a man, but a member, an instrument, a thing.

The report then went on to include a series of ten proposals. The primary or "keystone" of the Committee's report was the following resolution, Proposal #1:

> The Advisory Committee on Alternate Education recommends that all avenues within existing structures be examined in terms of programs to meet unmet needs, and that the district provide learning environments to meet those student needs that are not being met. A 'learning environment' is any setting, either in or out of the existing buildings, which provides opportunities to meet these students' unmet needs.

And their report included this Proposal #7:

> Recognizing that there is a need for continuing responsible assistance in the exploration, implementation, and evaluation of learning environments, the Committee recommends that an ongoing committee be established by the Board of Education that would include students, parents, and staff to assist in these functions.

Thus, the "New Program Planning Committee" was formed in

the summer of 1973 and composed of six members, including some from the previous "Advisory Committee on Alternate Education." They presented their report in November of 1973. It had a lavender cover page and became known more generally simply as the "Lavender Proposal." The "Lavender Proposal" opened with the following quote from a study done for the New York State Commissioner of Education calling for "Optional Learning Environments"—or "Ole!, celebrating differences" as he used to like to say—"Providing Optional Learning Environments in New York State Schools":

> Any educational system that seeks to permit every individual to achieve at his maximum potential must provide multiple options. At all levels of the system, choices need to be made to accommodate a wide variety of factors—parental preferences; students' needs, interests, preferred learning styles, and personal welfare; as well as the welfare of society. The goals of education that we accept to carry out the ultimate mission of the New York State educational system are not now being fully achieved by all students. While this is most obvious for many of those in lower socioeconomic groups in urban areas, it is also true for many others who are now not well served by the traditional programs in all schools.

It is fair to say that there were several factors creating a favorable climate for the creation of the New Junior High Program and these favorable factors and others are still with us if we look for them:

1. The parents and students of a fore-runner alternative program were anxious for such an opportunity to be re-kindled, and put pressure on the Ithaca

Administration and School Board (perhaps surprising to some, historically in public education, such pressure has proven to be one of the most effective means of lobbying district administrators and school board members for change as they often feel compelled to listen to their constituents as they should);

2. There was the recommendation of the "Alternate Education Committee" to the School Board;

3. There were existing community agencies working with young people in a variety of ways who could speak knowingly to the need for alternative education; and

4. There was support for alternative education from the New York State Commissioner of Education and the New York State Education Department.

As one might expect with any new program, we were subject to, not just one, but four different outside evaluations during our three year trial period, from September 1974 to June 1977. The initial evaluation was done by a five-member team from the School of Human Ecology of Cornell University, and by a research associate, Mary Agnes Hamilton, which resulted in the "First Year Evaluation Report-New Junior High Program 1974-75." Others included the "Report on the New Program, March 1977" done by the Ithaca Secondary Principals, the "Evaluation of the New Program 1975-76 for the Ithaca Junior High Students" by Dr. Eric Gardner, Senior Editor, Stanford Achievement Test and Professor of Education and Psychology, Syracuse University, and "Visitation Report on the New Junior High School Program, January 1977" by Dr. Robert King, Coordinator of Optional Programs, of the New York State Education Department. The major findings in these reports were essentially positive and include the following:

• From the first year report of Mary Agnes Hamilton

regarding Family Groups: "They [students interviewed] saw the teacher-counselor groups [Family Groups]as people making decisions, and as good and worthwhile. Student descriptions of what happened in these sessions included: discuss ways of changing the school; go on hikes; discuss schedules; discuss school meetings; make decisions; plan get-togethers." And regarding parent involvement: "Parent involvement in the education of their child was an important part of the New Program, and many parents interviewed felt that it was one of its successes. Three modes of parent participation in the education of their child can be distinguished. They were meetings [both with their student's Family Group Leader and larger, general meetings with parents/caregivers], socials, and correspondence [by phone, written reports, and in person]. Different modes appealed to the personal styles of different parents."

- From the March 1977 report prepared by the Ithaca Secondary Principals: "We believe that the evidence herein offered [in the reports of Gardner and King] is a positive indication that the goals in the three areas of the learning environment, academic achievement and personal development have been successfully attained. Thus, we are satisfied that the New Program has successfully completed its three-year trial period." . . . "The secondary school principals of the Ithaca City Schools submit the following recommendations:

  1. The full endorsement of alternate education as now functioning in the New Junior High Program as an on-going integral part of Ithaca's secondary schools.

  2. The expansion of the present junior high alternative school program (grades 7-9) to include

grades 10-12, in September, 1978. Planning for an alternative junior-senior high school program, 7-12, as well as deciding on its permanent location, in an adequate, self-contained facility, should begin immediately, March, 1977."

- From the Summary of. Dr. King's report: "The New Program evidences a number of strengths, among these are:

  1. The availability and use of community resources.
  2. Parent participation and support in the program.
  3. Student participation in planning, decision-making and evaluation.
  4. The informality and small class size that enhances personal communication by the teacher and pupil and allows for individualization of instruction.
  5. Flexibility of schedule, which permits a variety of courses and learning experiences for students of this age.
  6. Three years of practical experience in conducting an alternative school program.
  7. Certified staff and a number of volunteers who contribute freely of their time to making the program work."

- From the report of Dr. Gardner: "The data which have been assembled by the evaluator . . . indicate that the New Program is achieving its objectives with modest financial support. The students compare favorably with those in the other junior high schools and with the national norms in the basic skills as measured by the Stanford Achievement Test given city-wide in May, 1976. The students have a variety of offerings; they participate in planning their own program; they have opportunities which most use to develop social and personal responsibility; the classes are small and students receive much individual attention and feedback about their progress; and there is considerable parental involvement and participation. The New Program is meeting the need of a number of pupils for whom the regular junior high school program would be much less satisfactory."

I end this chapter on the New Junior High Program with the public appeal we made to the Ithaca City School Board at a special meeting on March 21, 1977 held in the cafétorium of Boynton Middle School with a standing room only crowd. I presented the following as it was reprinted in the editorial section of *The Ithaca New Times*:

> Since you now have before you two divergent sets of recommendations regarding the future of alternative secondary education in Ithaca—those of the superintendent and those of the secondary school principals—I should like to make that choice quite clear, honest and precise.
>
> On the one hand you could choose to recognize the genuinely different and demonstrated successful philosophy of alternative education presently in the New Program. And, you could choose to give that philosophy an adequate home by phasing the New Program out of its present location [the old NYSEG building on Court and Plain Streets] next year, while planning for an expansion to include a high school program—thus creating an alternative junior/senior high school (grades 7-12) in Ithaca, permanently housed in the high school complex.
>
> Or, on the other hand, you could choose to end alternative education in Ithaca's secondary schools by closing the present New Program building this summer

and creating a so-called 'department of alternative; at Dewitt Junior High School—which is more precisely defined merely as an expansion of the present DeWitt 'Needs-Based Program.' Should you choose the latter, you must see clearly that you are telling a significant minority of this Ithaca City School District—students, parents, teachers, administrators and other members of the community—that there is no room for a different philosophy of education in Ithaca's secondary schools; that there is no room for a different way of relating to young people as decision-makers, teaching them with different and varied methods; that there is no room for a different way for teachers and a principal to relate and work together, collectively rather than hierarchically; that there is no room for a different way of working cooperatively with parents as prime decision-makers in educating their children; and, that there is no room for teachers and students to reach out and actively involve a whole community of resources in their teaching and learning.

For we are all children of the broken dream— the dream of Thomas Paine, Martin Luther King, and so many others—the dream that this country, this small community of Ithaca, N.Y., would in fact really be a land of freedom, and liberty, and justice for all. Indeed, for all—for the Native Americans still living as second-class citizens, for the Blacks who are still oppressed, for the Chicanos whose labor we still exploit—for all the minorities, and most especially for our nations' children. It is truly a tragedy that our nation's young may well be the last minority ever to gain this freedom—not license, but genuine freedom with social responsibility—the last minority ever to experience this liberty; this justice for all, regardless of age, sex, race, color, class or religious creed.

Thus, I urge you to continue to uphold the rights of the minority in this community—young people, parents and teachers alike—who believe so strongly and have worked so hard to develop what we have come to know as an 'alternate secondary school' with its different philosophy, methods and approaches to teaching and learning. Indeed, in a democratic society which, although it makes its decisions based on the will of the majority, yet has established rights and processes to recognize, preserve and protect the minority—you can choose no other route than to give alternative secondary education a permanent home in the Ithaca City School District. Clearly, the decision is yours. Godspeed."

Following a thunderous standing ovation, and some deliberation among themselves, the School Board voted eight to one in agreement with my proposal, and that of the secondary school principals, to relocate NJHP to the E-building wing in Ithaca High School.

Discussion Questions

1. What local agencies (similar to those described in this chapter) do you have in your community that work with youth and might be allies?
2. What colleges or universities are located in your community or nearby that might be helpful?
3. What parents/caregivers of the students you hope to

serve might be helpful in approaching your district administration and/or school board?

4. What community organizations like those that were helpful to NJHP in Ithaca might be formed in your community—if they don't already exist—and subsequently be helpful?

5. How might you convince your administration and school board to form a study group similar to those involved in the creation of NJHP?

6. What professional educational evaluators might be contacted to help set up an evaluation plan for your alternative school in the making?

7. What support might exist in your state department of education?

8. Why do you want to create an alternative school anyway? And for whom?

Resources

- Democratic Consensus Decision-Making. There is one publication that has particularly helpful processes and strategies for making student and staff decisions democratically: *On Conflict and Consensus: A Handbook on Formal Consensus Decision-making*, by C. T. Lawrence Butler and Amy Rothstein, Food Not Bombs Publishing (www.consensus.net), 2nd Edition, 1991

- Democratic Problem Solving and Related Skills. The most helpful material I've used includes the work of Thomas Gordon, now carried on through Gordon Training International (www.gordontraining.com) and such publications as *Teacher Effectiveness Training (TET)*, *Leadership Effectiveness Training (LET)*, and their original book, *Parent Effectiveness Training (PET)*. These involve strategies and practice activities including "active listening," "I-messages," the "Six-Step Problem-Solving Process," and "Conflict-Resolution."

Chapter Two

From Junior High to High School

*W*ith the decision to move NJHP to Ithaca High
School, deliberations began to determine just
where in the sprawling, primarily one-story,
building we would be located. At a joint meeting of IHS and
NJHP staff in late March of 1977 consideration was given to
the second floor of "G-building," primarily housing the social
studies department, "K-building," primarily housing the foreign
language department, the "Activities Building" housing music
rooms and a large auditorium, and "E-building" housing drivers
education, special education, some offices, and the custodial and
receiving area. It was quickly determined that E-building would
be best. [One could have predicted that these non-academic
activities—drivers education and special education—would be
viewed as less important and chosen to move to another part of
the high school! And we probably shouldn't have been surprised
when in the late spring our first year in this wing of IHS, their
annual yearbook came out with the theme, "One less place to
go!—referring to our "school," complete with pictures taken
down our hall to introduce each section of the yearbook.] Thus,
the E-building wing, on the backside of IHS—just a few yards
from the school district's administration building, housing among
other key people, the superintendent, taking part of their parking
lot—became our new home.

There were two entrances to E-building, one down the long hall with the shop classrooms and student lockers on one wall, and the "back-door" to NJHP which was a little alcove off the parking lot. This quickly became the first choice for staff and students alike as the smoking area. We only had a couple of staff smokers and not many student smokers, however, technically that area was still on the school grounds. It was subsequently decided by students and staff that the smoking area would be moved a short distance across the parking lot to the sidewalk just outside E-building and the district administrative building. This wasn't the best view for people coming to our school, but since this only involved a few of our community, it seemed far better than students smoking in the bathrooms or the large courtyard outside the cafeteria, which is where the IHS students would sneak their smokes—or skip out of school altogether. This illustrates how these kinds of decisions and rule-making, which were made in discussion with our students, helped to break down the typical "we-they" between staff and students in most secondary schools.

Another issue discussed and resolved was the question of a "student lounge." Since there had been one at the old NJHP building on Court and Plain Streets, when we moved to E-building the students wanted a lounge, and with some of the renovations that were planned such a space seemed feasible, although with a large "bay window" that looked out on the entrance alcove to accommodate a pool table and ping pong table. Thus, it really was a "game-room/student lounge." However, this did not last long as we had to use the space for another teaching area given our growing enrollment. So the lounge was moved to an interior room—no pool or ping pong tables, no windows, and one door. This second lounge area in E-building soon became a lights-out, hang-out with some students "ruling-the-roost" so to speak. It became a hot topic at All School Meetings and was eventually turned into another room used for teaching, conferencing and/or counseling activities, with all agreeing that although having a lounge seemed a good idea, it did not really work well. Thus, the life of a student place to hang out between classes, moved to the hallways where they would gather quietly and in full view, a successful solution.

*****

Although the E-building wing was a better solution than the others initially proposed by the superintendent, it posed a new set of problems. In our old building we had ten classroom spaces and two office areas, and shared the building with no one else. E-building we shared with the four main industrial arts spaces down one side of the main corridor (where our students had their lockers)—the metal shop, auto shop, wood shop, and combined graphics, electricity, and small engine shop—and had only five potential classrooms, three small office spaces, and no nearby bathrooms of our own. Through active negotiations that spring we were able to have about $10,000 of renovations done, giving us our own bathrooms, three small office spaces, six teaching spaces, and the student lounge. Believing in the old adage—it's not how much space you've got, it's how you use the space you're given—we creatively redesigned E-building to house our middle-schoolers, who were of course eager to be in the "real" high school! And we did have limited access to their swimming pool—only certain hours and with proper supervision—part of their large dividable gym, a section of their playing fields, their cafeteria (for the late lunch), and library.

During the first year of the move of NJHP to the renovated E-building wing of IHS, the "Alternative Education Working Group" was convened to develop a plan for expanding the program to include an alternative high school, grades 10 through 12. This group submitted their Report to the Board of Education in February of 1978 with a proposal to add the high school grades to NJHP in and expansion of the NJHP space in IHS. Thus, in September of 1978 the "Alternative Community High School" (ACHS) with seventy-five 10th through 12th grade students joined the junior high students in E-building in only three additional classrooms around the corner and down the hallway across from the industrial arts classrooms. Two of these spaces were subsequently divided to create five actual teaching spaces and one office space.

Besides the need for adequate classroom spaces, there were two other needs—perhaps unique to our school—a meeting space large enough to accommodate the whole school, students and staff, and enough separate rooms for all of our Family Groups. These Groups typically ranged in size from 10 to 15, thus NJHP, having 60 students initially, needed six rooms for our Family Groups, and by using a couple of room-divider-curtains, we made it work. As for the large meeting space for our weekly All School Meetings, again we barely made it at the NJHP Court and Plain Street building, but made it work in a space at the end of the upstairs hallway, just outside the staff office with 70 some folding chairs. Having no gym of our own, we had an arrangement to use the gym, before the elementary schools were out, in GIAC (the Greater Ithaca Activities Center), a neighborhood center just across the street from NJHP and at the end of the block. Once in the E-building wing of IHS,[1] we were able to use some of their gym space, and created a meeting space for our All School Meetings by opening up the former drivers education classroom (which we had divided with a folding curtain into two smaller classrooms) to accommodate all the students and staff as we grew to over 100, often with several sitting on the floor.

In the five program recommendations of the "Working Group" it was envisioned that the high school students would have opportunities for "Career/Vocational Experiences" and "Community Studies," both of which would see students out in the greater Ithaca community in various real-world learning opportunities. One of the ways curriculum wise that the new high school staff thought this might be accomplished—thanks to an idea of our former NJHP bus driver/darkroom instructor, now a certified biology teacher—by making one day per week a "Project" day in which students would be out of the building in various interdisciplinary activities. This involved several of the staff and the coordination of considerable planning to implement, and was soon modified to be two, half-days rather than one full day (Tuesday afternoons and Thursday mornings), as we discovered that sustaining interest in one project for one whole day each week was more than students and staff found doable. Also, having these "Extended Projects" on two different days meant some could be the same project meeting twice a week, while others could be two different projects on those two days. This allowed our high school students to more fully utilize the assistance of the "Learning Web" for some of our community placements as well as the Ithaca Youth Bureau to expand some of the programs begun with our junior high students. We had hoped to have two mini-buses available to help with student access to these various community opportunities, but managed only free bus tickets for the city bus (there was a bus stop right outside our door), and the use of a donated station wagon.[2]

One particularly neat example of the first dozen or so "Extended Projects" was known as "The Danby Dig," and involved fifteen students. Here is a description of the project

1. Then there was the year when Fall Creek—which came over Ithaca Falls and by the south side of the IHS campus—flooded our E-building wing of the high school. There were several inches of water in our hallways and classrooms, and we had to be evacuated for several weeks. Fortunately we were able to move to GIAC and use several rooms there on a shortened schedule, while much of the rest of IHS was flooded (as well as Boyton Middle School which was just a playground's separation north, and flooded causing them to go to a split-day schedule sharing space at DeWitt Middle School), leaving the high school to find various locations to hold classes on a drastically reduced schedule.

from the booklet they subsequently published about their work, *Bald Hill Road: Glimpse into the Past*:

> This particular project began as an attempt to turn our interests in amateur archaeology toward the study of our own community. [Bald Hill is a road in the town of Danby which is part of the Ithaca School District located about seven miles south of Ithaca.] We spent eight Tuesdays in the field exploring Bald Hill Road's many foundations and cellar holes, choosing one to excavate, laying a three-meter grid and carefully removing the soil, rocks, and artifacts [200 pounds worth]. We partially restored an old well and found the foundations of a barn and a tool shed, as well as the remains of a root cellar or cistern. We found the remains of many objects, including scythe blades, crocks, canning jars, medicine bottles, tea cups, hundreds of square nails, pieces of a cast iron stove, spoons, knives, and other messengers of the past.
>
> The contents of this booklet are based [in addition to the actual "dig"] primarily on historical facts found through researching old journals, newspaper clippings, maps, and deeds [and interviews of senior citizens still living in the area]. These facts have been written out in a creative, fictional style in order to present them in such a way that the reader can visualize the lives of the people living at that time.

2. Initially anyone on our staff with a valid New York Driver's License could drive the car, and we had it filled with gas and serviced at the school bus garage, and parked it in the lot outside E-building. Students thought it was great fun to pile-in a Family Group and go to Purity Ice Cream just a few blocks away. But soon it was discovered—remember the parking lot was shared with district administrators—that it was supposed to meet NY Department of Transportation inspection regulations to transport students, and of course, although safe, it did not meet these regulations, thus we lost our station wagon.

These Extended Project days also made scheduling of rehearsals for our drama groups more accessible to more students, meeting all morning on Thursdays and in the afternoons on Tuesdays. Over the years LACS became known for outstanding drama productions, typically involving a middle school play and a high school play each year as well as some one act plays and improvisationals put on at the annual Spaghetti Dinner. We struggled to find appropriate stage space and used the auditorium at the Greater Ithaca Activities Center, the Beverly J. Martin Elementary School stage, the Ithaca Community Playhouse down town, even local churches, as well as a theatre space at Cornell University, Ithaca High School's theatre, and one of the outstanding high school productions, "Dead Poet's Society" which was held in the newly renovated Hangar Theatre (it originally had been a small hangar for private planes) in Cass Park. Our Middle School dramas included all students who were interested, and sometimes involved writing in some new small parts to include more performers, or a production of "Alice in Wonderland" which involved three different Alices taking turns throughout the show! Productions included musicals with students providing the appropriate instrumental background, and even involved yours truly in some cameo appearances, e.g as Mr. Bumble in "Oliver Twist," and Officer Krupke in "West Side Story." Upon moving to West Hill we were able to turn our own "Band-Box Gym" into the "Black Box Theatre" with a fully equipped theater area for drama and music productions, complete with risers for seating, and a full sound and lighting system, adding a full-size gym. Subsequently we held an all-school community build, creating the "Outdoor Amphitheater," also for drama and musical productions. Several times over the years, senior high school students wrote their own original plays which were then put on by the students. Thus it can be seen that drama has always been a big part of the curriculum at LACS involving

students in working collaboratively toward a common goal—
making sets and customs, managing the lighting, sometimes
learning to dance and/or sing, designing the programs, and
managing the refreshments at intermission.

There were other curricular experiments involving another
one of the five program recommendations of the "Working
Group;" what we called "Cottage Industries." One was a silk-
screen t-shirt shop which not only made t-shirts for the school,
but also for other customers in the Ithaca community. We
also utilized IHS's Graphics Shop to produce an alternative
education magazine, the *Alternative Schools Exchange: The
Unicorn*, to which we sold subscriptions and distributed
nationally for three years. Jonathan Kozol described the
magazine in his book, *Alternative Schools: A Guide for
Educators and Parents*, as the "best politically oriented
newsletter on alternative education, with quarterly publication,
book reviews, and curriculum resources." The students chose
themes for each issue, solicited articles from various alternative
schools and authors throughout the country, researched
resources to recommend to our readers, printed, collated,
addressed and mailed copies to lists of subscribers from other
independent alternative education magazines that were ending
their publications.[3]

Enrollment in NJHP/ACHS continued to grow each
year, and the sixth grade was added when the Ithaca District
went to a middle school model (grades 6 through 8 with the
elementary schools becoming pre-K through 5th grades, and
the high school becoming grades 9 through 12). Although now
serving as Principal of the whole program, grades 6 through 12,
I continued to teach a science and health class each semester,
including a popular one—"Dogs and Cats"—which came as
a request from some of the younger students who had pets at
home.[4]

The curriculum was now structured into four nine-week

cycles for both junior high and high school students (plus the one week in the spring for the camping trip) with seven periods of 45 minutes each per day. Classes, mini-courses, community projects, or open labs were scheduled for various numbers of periods per week—some meeting one period every day of the week, others meeting two, three, or four periods per week, or for two to three periods back-to-back one, two, or three times per week—all depending on the nature of the learning activity and the students' needs. The on-going process by which the specific components of the curriculum were developed for each seven-week cycle was intended to help students develop the power over, and responsibility for, their own education. This involved the following steps:

1. The process began during the last two weeks of each cycle when cards were given to each student and staff member to indicate what they would like to learn during the next cycle, as well as what they would like to teach or assist in teaching.

3. From the late 1960s to the 1980s there were at least 18 alternative education magazines, including such grassroots publications as: *Applesauce*, (published by the National Alternative Schools Program out of the University of Massachusetts, ending in 1980); the *New Schools Exchange Newsletter* (140 issues, ended in 1978. Judy and I worked with the NSEN collective on an organic farm, Shanti Gardens, outside Columbus, Ohio for two and a half years); *Edcentric: A Journal of Educational Change* (from Eugene Oregon, ended in the 70s); *This Magazine Is About Schools* (from Canada until late 70s); *Changing Schools: The Journal of Alternative Education* (from 1973 until late 1980s out of Boulder, Colorado); *Centerpeace: A Free School Magazine* (serving the New England area); *The Innovative Education News* (from New Orleans area); *Return to Learning* (out of Fort Wayne, Indiana); *Alternatives for Education* (from San Pedro, California); and the *Teacher Drop-Out Center* (initially out of Cambridge, Massachusetts and later out of Ithaca College in Ithaca, New York).

4. I was particularly surprised and pleased to learn from one of the students in this course who spoke with me just a couple of years ago at the school's 40th anniversary; that thanks to that class, he had been able to save the life of his pet cat years later. The cat had been struck by a car, and although not breathing, did not seem to have sustained a death blow, and because this former student had learned in the course how to deliver artificial respiration to a dog or cat, he was able to get the cat breathing again, and thus save its life!

2. Parents/caregivers were notified of an open meeting to get their input for the next cycle and list of possible things they might like to teach or assist in teaching.
3. A master list of possible classes, mini-courses, community projects, or open labs (usually numbering well over 100) was then distributed to all students to indicate their possible interests.
4. A Curriculum Committee of staff, students, and parents/caregivers then formed this list of preferences into a master schedule with a course booklet describing each activity, whether new or continuing from the previous cycle.
5. Each Family Group Advisor (Teacher-Counselor) then held a conference with each of the their students in conjunction with their parents/caregivers (sometimes done simply by phone) to formulate a learning program or contract for the next nine-week cycle.

Some of the curriculum offerings included course titles such as in Communications Arts/English:

> Classic Adventure Stories
> Crunch English
> Creative Writing
> Poetry
> Reading Hour
> Biography and Autobiography
> Spelling and Vocabulary
> Theatre Appreciation
> Mythology
> Medieval Literature
> Oral History Project
> Linguistics

Women's Readings
Sports Heroes
Russian Literature
Television & Other Media
Recent Writers
Science Fiction

In Social Studies:

Afro-American History
World Geography
Basic Social Studies Skills
Medieval History
Law and Courts
Changing Roles of Men & Women
U.S. Geography

In Science:

Chemistry
Astronomy
Field Studies
Wood, Water, and Wind (alternative energy)
Animal Dissection
African Animals
Marine Biology
Physics

In Health:

Human Sexuality
Nutritional Foods
Healing: Herbs, Balms, etc.

Advanced First Aid
Psychology

In Mathematics:

Basic Skills
Enrichment I
Enrichment II
Algebra 9
Algebra 9a (2 year)
Algebra II
Math for Life
Math Games in Open
Math Lab (Othello, Chess, Yahtze, etc.)

In Foreign Language:

Spanish I
Spanish II
French I
French II
German I
German II

In Physical Education:

Ice Skating
Bowling
Gymnastics
Volleyball
Weight Room
Hiking
Developmental Gym
Swimming

In Art:

Basic Drawing
Pottery
Clay
Batik
Nature Crafts
Chalk Drawing
Water Colors
Sewing
Macrame
Mural Painting

In Music:

Chorus
Guitar
Music Theory
Music Appreciation

Additionally, that first group of high school students, although technically graduating with an Ithaca High School diploma, wanted their graduation to mean something special and different from the IHSers. Thus, it was proposed and approved overwhelmingly at a meeting of our high school students that each of them would do an individual "Senior Graduation Project." They developed some simple guidelines requiring a brief proposal to be accepted by a student/staff committee and that each project would be presented at the graduation ceremony. Our first high school graduation saw some wonderfully diverse presentations including:

- An extensive diary that had been kept all year describing one of our young women's experience working weekly with a senior citizen; she was initially interested in going into geriatrics as a college student, but after this intensive experience in a local senior center, decided not to pursue that as a career;

- A totally re-built Camarro convertible car done by a student who's father owned a local truck repair shop; he drove the car, freshly re-upholstered and re-painted inside and out, to graduation;

- Similarly, another senior totally re-built the engine and re-painted a motorcycle, drove it to graduation, and subsequently rode it on a tour of the U.S. after graduation;

- A scarf, gloves, and hat knitted from yarn that had been prepared from raw wool, including learning to card, spin, dye, and weave the yarn;

- A full-size handmade, navigable, wooden canoe;

- A small handmade sailboat, "The Pumpkin Seed," also navigable;

- More than one concert of original music on a guitar, on a cello, on the piano, and on the violin;

- A booklet published about the life of Fred Briehl, a World War I conscientious-objector, by one of our young men who was seriously considering being a conscientious-objector

This last item—actually a 30-page pamphlet/booklet—was the first of a series of publications we called, *Ox Prints: Occasional Papers of ACS* with a drawing of footprints of an Ox on the cover. You ask, "why an Ox?" Early that first year of the combined New Junior High Program and Alternative Community High School—quite a mouthful and too long to really use as the name of our school—we decided on the shorter "Alternative Community School" or "ACS," which we subsequently pronounced "Ox!" Then, remembering the legendary story of Paul Bunyan and his Blue Ox, "Babe," who strolled across the Midwest leaving big footprints and creating the Great Lakes, I pointed out that we, too, intended to make a deep and lasting impression as well, leaving "Ox prints," not only in New York, but all over the country! And the Ox became our mascot and was quickly illustrated by one of our young artists, and a large Ox head was soon painted on the door of the former Industrial Arts office in E-building, much to the disapproval of the department chairman and high school principal.

Although there were some sixteen "Goals" outlined in the original "Report of the New Program Planning Committee" in November of 1973, because they had not been generated by the students, staff, and parents/caregivers, they actually received little real attention, other than to make sure they would be addressed in the evaluation reports of the outside consultants described in the first chapter. These Goals fell into three categories:

1. Four general goals pertaining to setting up the learning environment and its maintenance, for instance, "to establish a learning environment characterized by openness, honesty, confidence and mutual trust;"
2. Eight pertaining to academic success, such as "to provide an extensive range of learning experiences;" and
3. Four involved with personal development, for example "to help each student become a self-directed and independent learner." For each of these sixteen Goals there were one or more "Strategies for Attainment." For example, a strategy accompanying the Goal just given in category 3) "by involving the student in the identification, shaping and management of much of his [her] learning environment."

These were all laudable goals with thoughtful strategies, yet again, they did not emerge from the context of, nor the direct involvement of, the initial participants in the New Junior High Program.

Thus, one of our seniors in our second year in E-building, for her senior project did a survey of students and staff and came up with the following nine statements—which she subsequently had framed and presented at graduation—of just what the Alternative Community High School [note that intentionally did not include NJHP] was all about:

1. "Creates a supportive community,
2. Provides an alternative to traditional education,
3. Provides a flexible government in which all may participate,
4. Is flexible enough to change with the needs of the community,
5. Provides an education which is relevant to the individual,
6. Breaks down barriers between teachers and students,
7. Provides opportunity for individuals to use their creativity,
8. Teaches environmental concern and social awareness, [because]
9. The intent of this school is to be educational, personal, and FUN!"

This certainly was a more apt description of what we all hoped was actually happening, particularly for our high school component which was just in its second year. Then, in 1977, upon a visit from an alternative educator whom I met at one of the national alternative education conferences (I also visited his alternative program, the Dome Project out of New York City) and at his suggestion staff and students developed the following "Mission Statement" and "Goals" for the combined junior-senior high school, ACS:

Mission

- To educate students to be global citizens in the 21st century.

Goals

1. To be a genuine Alternative where:
   a. Students, staff, and parents/caregivers are directly involved in governance;
   b. Students have opportunities for personal interaction with many adults, both in school and in the community;
   c. Students may study subjects of personal interest;
   d. Students are involved in anti-racist/anti-bias education; and
   e. Courses are available which relate to contemporary issues in society.
2. To be a cooperative, supportive Community striving to share power and resources within the school and the larger community.
3. To be a School, an environment for active teaching and learning, working and playing together.
4. To remain steadfastly responsive to the people who make up our school community and, thus, to adapt to the changing needs of our students, parents/caregivers, and staff.
5. To encourage respectful relationships among people of different age, economic, racial, cultural and ethnic groups, providing opportunities to learn from each other, both academically and socially.

6. To provide curriculum and instruction which is non-competitive, heterogeneously grouped, and has constructive evaluation based on individual learning.
7. To provide a staff that is at least as diverse as the student body, providing role models and support for all students.
8. To encourage personally relevant expression and communication through the universal language of the arts.
9. To provide a curriculum that helps each student improve skills, from grade six through twelve, enabling each graduate to go on with education, to enter the job market, and to meet problems of daily life.
10. To provide appropriate support to help each student grow in skills, whatever the ability or subject.
11. To help students learn about their emotional, as well as intellectual and physical, selves.
12. To teach non-violent conflict resolution.
13. To act as a resource and forum for sharing our educational experiences within our district and beyond.

In the spring of 1987, a joint student and staff and parent/caregiver "Committee to Re-evaluate and Re-vitalize the Curriculum" was created, and one of their tasks was to develop a statement of philosophy[5] for ACS (see chapter five for more about this important work):

The Lehman Alternative Community School's philosophy is based on certain beliefs and ideals. We recognize that change in our world is inevitable and we believe that it can be directed to promote the common welfare. Therefore, as an educational institution:

- We believe we have a responsibility to promote a

broader world view and a positive change by the way we design our curriculum and prepare our students for learning throughout their lives.

- We believe in the importance of each individual student.
- We believe in encouraging students to use freedom responsibly, and to make educational choices appropriate to their individual levels of development.
- We believe in providing for the needs of a diverse population of students, and students of all abilities.
- We believe in a fair, caring, community-run school with respectful consciousness of all minorities.
- We believe each student can excel through self-discipline, community support, and respect for people of all ages as educators and fellow learners.
- We believe that learning can be of value to students in their present lives, not just for the future, and that students have a place in, and can make contributions to their society.
- We believe the affective and creative aspects of learning are as valuable as objective and conceptual learning.
- We believe, as a caring community, we will be concerned about recycling, reusing, composting, conserving energy, and feeding ourselves with locally-grown food.[6]

By acting on these beliefs and ideals, we can enable our children to deal positively with change and to

5.   This was reviewed and revised by the Alternative Community School community during the 1995-96 school year. It is the revised form which appears here and continued after the school was re-named the Lehman Alternative Community School in the spring of 2004, appearing on panels posted in the LACS gym.

contribute constructively both socially and politically to society.

Early in the school's history (following a visit to Central Park East school in East Harlem) we listed in the *Footbook*, and began working with our students on five "Habits of Mind." These were:

1. Asking "how do we know what we know?";
2. Seeing through multiple viewpoints;
3. Imagining alternatives by asking "what if?";
4. Seeing/making connections; and
5. Asking "what difference does it make?'"

These then led to developing five "Habits of Behavior" which we asked and expected students to do:

1. Sharing responsibility for group work;
2. Keeping personal records of your learning;
3. Saving and organizing your work;
4. Being on time; and
5. Getting things completed on time.

Then, in the summer of 1994, the "Families Against Racism" (with parent/caregiver, staff, and student representatives) developed a list of what are to be expected that "An LACS Person of Character Strives to Be," and after being reviewed by the school community, were approved by the LACS Site Based Council in June of 1996:

---

6. This belief statement was added in 2004, acknowledging the work that had been going on for some time initially by students in the Ecology class, and expanded to include others helping with the different components involved in the recycling.

- Anti-Biased: accepting others and their differences, realizing how their actions affect others.
- Responsible: by acting in accordance with school guidelines and philosophy, and being drug, alcohol, and tobacco free on school grounds, trips, and all other LACS activities.
- Respectful: listening to others, acknowledging individuals merits and rights to make decisions, avoiding abuse, mistreatment, or taking advantage of people or their mistakes.
- Trustworthy: demonstrating honesty, integrity, and reliability.
- Caring: being kind, sharing, and sensitive to the feelings of others.

Though these habits and qualities of character were never formally assessed or evaluated, they were deemed critical to develop and important throughout each student's school experience.

Throughout those early years the staff needed to work closely and to know each other well, as we ran the school organizationally as a horizontal collective, sharing in all the decisions, which required what I'm sure some felt were endless meetings once a week, every Wednesday afternoon after school from 2:45pm until 5:00 or 5:30pm. With help from one of our parents/caregivers experienced in group process—we developed a process for these weekly meetings which involved splitting the time equally between "staffing"—discussing how we could help specific students who were having difficulty being successful—and "business," all that was involved in planning everything that happened in running the school from day to day, week to week. As we were still working out the combination of the junior and senior high programs, these "business meetings" were with separate junior and senior high staff the 1st, 2nd, and 3rd weeks of each month, with the 4th Wednesday for a combined meeting. The "staffing" part of the meetings were divided into junior high staffing the 1st and 3rd Wednesdays, and the senior high staffing the 2nd and 4th Wednesdays. We also had staff workshops during the last week in August before school began in September and on district "professional development days," at least once or twice per school year. Again with help from other alternative educators met at conferences, we developed a 7-step decision-making process for staff meetings involving:

1. Identification of the problem
2. Clarification
3. Data gathering
4. Hypotheses – how 'bouts
5. Opinions, feelings, refinement
6. Consensus proposals
7. Consensus

And agreed on the following processes to help us use the time well in making decisions:

1. organize for overall meeting to:
   a. Prioritize agenda
   b. Watch time, avoid tangents
   c. Move to decision
   d. Elicit responses
2. Information-giver, chair for sub-sections—come prepared, use graphics, write-out decisions on chalkboard or newsprint
3. Rotate leaders with encouragement for those for whom this will be new
4. Feedback for leader at end of each meeting

5. Note-taker/recorder—e.g. last week's chair
6. "Follow-up-er"—this week's chair sees that decisions are carried out

Clearly, one of the main things involved in being a democratic school is for staff to fully embrace all that this implies and getting up to speed with the processes involved. This was particularly challenging for new staff each year, and it sometimes helped to pair the new folks with those who had been at ACS several years already.

With all of these democratic processes well in hand, and an ever expanding enrollment, we now needed a larger space. In a cost saving measure in 1979, the School Board closed four elementary schools, selling three and keeping West Hill Elementary School with some of its space being rented by a small private elementary school and a large classroom being leased by a pre-k/day-care program. ACS was subsequently moved to West Hill. Many changes occurred along the way with our use of this building which early on became our own home as the private elementary school moved to another location, and the pre-k program moved to one of the elementary schools downtown.

The biggest building change in 2008—four years after I retired—was the student-and-staff-designed expansion of LACS, with a new wing attached to the east side of the building with an enclosed glass walkway attaching the two. This now includes three fully-equipped science labs (a far cry from that converted science room in the original NJHP where I did the infamous raccoon dissection!). There is an expanded, fully-equipped kitchen with a student cafeteria eating area where the old kitchen and a classroom formerly were. There now is a full-sized gymnasium with locker rooms in a new wing, replacing our former, tiny "band-box" gym with the "Black Box Theater." The Band-Box Gym was also directly above the library which made "quiet study" a challenge for students and staff alike. It, too, was changed with the addition of the new wing, and now is a separate music area with three sound-proof practice rooms and a large central space for various music groups to practice.

And then there's our real library! Originally when we were in the former NJHP building on the corner of Court and Plain Streets, "our" library was the Tompkins County Library, two blocks down Court Street. Then, upon moving initially into the West Hill building we were told by the administration that we would not have a library. However, we divided one of the larger classrooms into a smaller classroom space with the beginning of our own library with shelves we scrounged and some of the sixth grade books left from the days when it was an elementary school, and using some of our own funds for new reference materials. This space also served initially as the "Hardback Café," where at lunch time every other week we would have a guest musician—student, staff, parent/giver, and/or guests playing music during lunch [even including myself with my old Gibson guitar and folk/rock repertoire!]. We eventually were able to convince the district that we indeed needed our own library and moved from that room to that space under the gym, which also housed the "School Store"— originally constructed by a group of students and a teacher— which was student-run offering school supplies and snack items (subsequently not considered proper by the district Cafeteria Manager as it "competed" with the school lunch program which still was being brought up from one of the other middle school kitchens).

With the construction of 2008, the library now moved into an amazing space, as part of the new wing, with study tables and reading areas, computer terminals, a separate classroom space fully-equipped for computer-based instruction, and the east side totally windows with an incredible view of the south end of Cayuga Lake and the Inlet, downtown Ithaca, and the Cornell University campus on East Hill. Early in our years at West Hill, there also had been a great need for extra storage space, and thus a large storage trailer was "parked" on the school grounds and used primarily for the sets for our drama productions. With the addition of the new wing, this was taken care of with a storage area included. Thus, the LACS building continues to change, new things are added to the school grounds and/or the physical building in which the teaching/learning occurs, believing that every number of years such projects give each succeeding generation of students "ownership" of their school.

Besides all of these valuable parts of the different buildings we lived in, there was/is the need for a number of offices. In the original NJHP building this space was at a real premium. We essentially had one staff office with several desks, including mine, in a less-than-private space with a half-glass divider wall which made it tough for our school psychologist (who came part of a day once a week, primarily to do testing for possible special ed classification), or our social worker (who also came once a week), our half time guidance counselor (the other half of her time as our Spanish teacher), to hold any kind of private conversation, and our school nurse (who came two half days per week). Our secretary had a desk behind a reception counter in the front entrance way, and our part-time custodian (who also was our school bus driver and ran the darkroom in one end of our supply/storage room) kept his things in a corner of the boy's/men's room. When we moved to the E-building wing of IHS the secretary still had a desk behind the reception counter, now in the back entryway, and I did have a small office of my own as did our guidance counselor, while our social worker and psychologist shared another office. We didn't have our own part-time nurse, but had access to the IHS nurse in another part of the high school building.

Then, initially upon moving to, and sharing, the West Hill

building, I had my own office, behind the office of our School Secretary, and off of her office there now was a staff bathroom. Having added a special education teacher to our staff, she had her own room, which doubled as a meeting space for the weekly meetings of both our "Curriculum Coordinators" (with a staff member from each of the major subject areas) and our "Support Team" (principal, social worker, school psychologist, guidance counselor, and nurse) which primarily did weekly "Case Reviews" of students who were not succeeding. This Team also included our "Outreach Worker" from the Ithaca Youth Bureau who worked particularly with our students who, some might say, had "behavioral issues." Besides receiving extra tutoring and counseling, these students were in a "Nature and Survival" group which did outdoor activities once a week for a half or full day, from rock-climbing to back-packing and tent-camping. Occasionally our outreach worker would take a student out of school for a day and do intensive one-to-one counseling to help the student get back on track. We, also, now had a full-time custodian who was assigned to our building, and after two changes of "assigned" custodians, a custodian from one of the elementary schools volunteered to be our custodian. Now, over 20 years later, he has a new assignment and title, "Dean of Students," which is what he really had been doing all along, getting to know the students, counseling with them, keeping his ear to the ground, and keeping a lid on things when they seemed like they might get out of hand.

Over the years in our different locations there has been the question of handicap access. Originally in the initial NJHP building, the first floor was a ground floor and thus students only had access to that level of classrooms, but in those first three years we had no students who were in a wheel chair or on crutches. Then, in the E-building wing, since IHS was basically all on the ground floor, there was no need for special handicap access other than a wooden ramp we built at the curb coming off of the parking lot. However, once at West Hill, other than a sloping asphalt sidewalk around the north side of the building—which really was not workable for a wheel chair—and a ramp we built into the gym from the sidewalk which had a curb cut from the parking lot, there really was not adequate handicap access. An elevator was built into what had been a small storage/file room on the lower level and a kitchen storage room on the upper level. A kitchen storage space subsequently was built just outside the kitchen to the north of the building. Now our building is fully handicapped accessible and we have had a number of students requiring and using these facilities.

*****

The LACS Support Team – an Essential Component

In addition to the physically handicapped students just referred to, from the beginning LACS always had a number of "students with special needs," those technically identified as "learning disabled." Over the years there have been, and continue to be, great staff devoted to working particularly with these young people. These professionals have been incorporated in all aspects of the program, with our special education teachers and teaching assistants often joining in the classrooms, helping teachers appropriately modify their teaching to be mindful of these students. One of our long-time special education teachers offered a horseback riding program during Extended Project afternoons, and this seemed to be particularly effective with some of our most challenged students. There was something special that happened when these students learned not only how to ride, but how to care for the horses. The special education teachers, too, were fully a part of the school, including co-leading Spring Trips in cross-country hiking and camping group, kayaking, and building at "Children's Garden" in one of the city parks.

We also have had students who were "English Language Learners" (ELL), or students with "English as a Second Language" (ESL). LACS seemed to offer a particularly effective learning environment for these youngsters who came from many countries including from Laos, Cambodia, Vietnam, and South American countries and others since Ithaca was a sanctuary city serving many of those fleeing political persecution and violence. Perhaps because LACS is such a highly verbal place with a focus on relationships, these students were immersed in conversations with their peers with English as their first language. Our approach was to involve them in everything—just like with our special needs students—all aspects of our program. Our ESL Teacher met additionally with them individually and also in small groups to work on their English. And their parents and caregivers were included as part of our greater community. I sometimes held meetings just with them and our ESL teacher and a native speaker/translator at a public assistance/neighborhood housing center where many of them lived. Unfortunately, later in our history, with a change in district central administration the LACS ESL program was discontinued due to the different view of how best to serve this population, which was to combine all of them in one school.

From our early days at NJHP with a part-time counselor/part-time Spanish teacher, LACS has had outstanding guidance counselors who do not have the typical role of "scheduler," devoting most of their time to scheduling students at the beginning of each term. Instead our counselors actually counsel students, one counselor working primarily with middle school students and one with high schoolers. Thus they do not have a Family Group, and don't oversee a Committee, but do coordinate the administration of any district or state required standardized tests while participating fully in Spring Trips and all other school functions. They also meet with students individually, and assist Family Group leaders as necessary.

We shared our original part-time social worker with Ithaca High School. She met effectively with parents/caregivers and was a member of our Advisory Board. I recall well in our first year when an active member of an ultra-conservative group was hell-bent on shutting down NJHP and tried to enroll her son. Our social worker was particularly effective with her "de-advertising/down-playing," what many at the time called, "The Alternate," leading this parent to withdraw her application. Our more recent social worker was responsible for developing, and overseeing, the WAM ("Welcoming Allies and Mentors") program (see Chapter 3).

Over the years our different school psychologists have been valuable contributors to our program, often providing individual and small-group counseling for some of our most needy students, as well as a helpful resource to our Family Group leaders. The school psychologists provide not only the mandated testing for students being special education classified, they provide much valuable insight at our weekly Support Team meetings. They, too, participate fully in all the various aspects of our program.

Although in the early years we did not have our own full-time school nurse, each of our part-timers brought a gracious, welcoming, kindness in caring for the medical needs of our students, as well as staff, including myself. There was even a parent who was a fully certified nurse who joined us on the spring camping trips in those early years of NJHP. In later years, our full-time nurse was particularly helpful to some of our most needy special education students, providing a comfortable place for them to drop by and hangout on their free time. And again, like all our Support Team members, our nurse participated fully in all aspects of the program, such as coordinating our winter ski program, with staff and students from Ithaca High School.

Thus, I could easily devote a whole chapter to the very special place and crucial roles played by all the professional members of our Support Team.

*****

A school garden—and subsequently a small green house—at West Hill were also developed and managed by our science teachers and student volunteers. With the expansion of the school building this subsequently was moved to its present location, now enclosed with a fence, and housing a student-built storage shed. In addition there has been a large organic garden project started on some land just south of Ithaca. With the forward-thinking leadership of one of the LACS science teachers, and subsequently two local organic farm collectives (Full Plate and Stick and Stone), and the Southside Community Center, all created a summer job experience for youth ages 14-18 that exemplifies what it means to work together, learn leadership and communication skills, and learn to grow food organically for the Ithaca community. A core part of the program is bringing youth together from diverse social and economic backgrounds, giving them responsibility in all aspects of farm work, from planting seeds to selling the produce at market stands they manage themselves. Located on 10 acres, each year they grow 4-5 acres in annual vegetable crops, managing the other 5-6 acres in cover crops such as red clover, rye or alfalfa. The food they grow goes to: the LACS lunch program (which now offers a student-run salad bar at lunch), the Ithaca City School District Lunch Program, the Full Plate Farm Collective CSA ("Community Supported Agriculture"—growing their u-pick garden), Beverly J. Martin Elementary School's Fresh Fruit and Vegetable Snack

Program, Greater Ithaca Activities Center, and the Congo Square Market (Friday evenings in the summer at Southside Community Center). "The Fresh Snack Program," now a farm-to-school program of The Youth Farm Project, announced that the 305 students in Caroline Elementary began receiving fresh classroom snacks in the fall of 2016, becoming the fourth elementary school to benefit from the program in Ithaca City School District (ICSD). The Fresh Snack Program now serves 1,230 pre-K through 5th grade students in the four ICSD elementary schools with highest indicator rates for family poverty. An additional snack bowl is also prepared each school day for the students in Southside Community Center's afterschool program.

Lastly, outdoor/playground space has also been a need wherever we've been housed. Initially at the NJHP building there was a small city park next to our building with a basketball court, a softball field, and additional open playground space. We also had arrangements with GIAC (the Greater Ithaca Activities Center neighborhood facility) to use their indoor basketball court. When we were in the E-building wing of IHS we had access to some of their fields including tennis courts, but the problem was coordinating our interests with the high school's PE classes. And this was the same situation with access to a section of their large gymnasium and their indoor swimming pool, although we did manage to find times and made it work. The West Hill building – being on a "hill" as the name indicates—provided its own set of challenges to find useable, somewhat level, playground space, but it was great for Frisbee, one of our students' favorite games/sport. A small asphalt playground—which also doubled as a staff parking lot—did have a basketball court. The large gymnasium, which was part of the building expansion, has been a welcome part of the new addition. Not having our own athletic facilities for more than 30 initial years of our history, did not stop many of our students from becoming interscholastic athletes. Throughout the years we had students who ran track, were on the swim team, the volleyball, basketball, baseball and football teams, and several were team captains and outstanding players.

Discussion Questions

1. Start by talking with those students and parents/caregivers about what they are hoping a different, "alternative" school might be, and with those who think they would like to be on the staff of such a school.
2. What grades should it include? High school 9-12? Middle school 6-8? Both 6-12? Elementary K-5? All grades, pre-K-12?
3. What kind of building—or portion of a building—will you need? Where can you find it? Does your school district own it? If not, will they lease it for your alternative school?
4. From the first meeting of possibly interested students and parents/caregivers, what are other questions unique to your school district that you'll need to answer?

Resources

Books about other alternative schools:

- *To Become Somebody: Growing Up Against the Grain of Society* (the story of the "Dome Project" in the Bronx) by John Simon, Houghton Mifflin Co., Boston, 1982;
- *Public Schools That Work: Creating Community*, edited by Gregory Smith, Routledge, 1993;

- *Against the Current: How One School Struggled and Succeeded with At-Risk Teens* (about the Urban Collaborative Accelerated Program in Providence, Rhode Island), by Michael Brosnan and Founding Principal, Rob DeBlois, Heinemann, 1997;
- *Making High School Work: Lessons from the Open School* (Jefferson County Open School in Colorado – a.k.a. "Mountain Open") by Tom Gregory, Teachers College Press, 1993;
- *Schools That Work: America's Most Innovative Public Education Programs* by George Wood (Former Principal, Federal Hocking High School, Athens, Ohio), Penguin Books, 1993;
- *How to Grow a School: Starting and Sustaining Schools That Work by Chris Mercogliano* (Former Director, The Free School, Albany, New York), Oxford Village Press, 2006;
- *The BIG Picture: Education Is Everyone's Business* by Dennis Littky (Director and Co-founder of the Metropolitan Regional Career and Technical Center – a.k.a. "The Met") with Samantha Grabvelle (Assistant to the Director at The Met), ASCD, 2004;
- *The Hardest Questions Aren't on the Test: Lessons from an Innovative Urban School* (Boston Arts Academy) by Linda Nathan (Founding Principal), Beacon Press, 2009

Chapter Three
Teaching Democratically

*I*n those first three years when we were still the New Junior High Program and had an enrollment of 65-85 students we took a week-long, "All School Spring Camping Trip." This involved all the students (there were a few exceptions—those with part-time jobs they could not miss, or were on spring sports teams and couldn't miss games held during Trips Week) and all of the staff. Spring Trips has been an integral part of our teaching and learning experience since the school began, and the purpose essentially is community building. It is important to our curriculum in many ways, allowing us to explore the community as our classroom—a chance to get off campus together. Adults and young people work together to make a trip happen, learning from each other, solving problems together. It transforms relationships by helping us get to know each other in different situations. It provides new challenges, teaching what it means to persevere, and opportunities to make lasting new friendships. Our alumni often name their Trip experiences as one of the most meaningful parts of their alternative education experience.

Preparation for Trips really began early in January with a number of fund-raising events, which initially involved selling raffle tickets—this was before such fund-raising by schools was deemed illegal by the New York State Department of Education. The monies raised were used originally to cover food, travel, and camping fees. The All School Camping Trip typically went down south to the Blue Ridge Mountains and National Park camp grounds. We were organized into small base camps of approximately ten (actually our Family Groups, which you'll learn more about in Chapter 4). It was in these smaller groups that the tent sleeping was arranged as well as cooking and eating, and most of the activities planned for each day (hikes to local points of interest, a soft ball game, capture-the-flag, nature walks, and just hanging-out in base camp).

Spring Trips thus became the locus of a number of special experiences, forming the sources of many fond memories. There was the year in the Blue Ridge Mountains of Virginia when I awoke with my base-campers in the middle of the night to shine a flashlight on not one, but an entire family of skunks foraging under the evergreen tree just a few yards outside the front flaps of our tent! There was the year when it rained virtually every day of the trip and on the final day—waiting for the school buses to arrive and take us, sopping-wet, home—we built a large drying rack for sleeping bags around a fire, and for those several hours I, and one of the staff, used up the as yet un-eaten, large #10 cans of corn, making them with the left-over flour, into fried corn-fritters, liberally dowsed in left-over syrup. And who could forget our visit on the last night down in Pennsylvania as we closed our emotional, community-building campfire—I always brought my guitar for funny and poignant sing-along songs, and handed-out a gift walking stick I'd carved during the week—hearing the rustling sounds of a mother black bear and her cubs, skirting the outer edges of our campsite looking for food we may have left out. Or, my most "painful" memory of the reservoir campsite where there was a large grassy hill leading down to the lake created by the dam, and one sunny afternoon after days of rain and an early morning shower, when I and one of the male high schoolers could see that it would be great fun to slide down the still damp grassy slope into the lake, never suspecting that part way down there would be a broken bottle buried part-way in the ground.

That activity quickly was halted as we came back up hill with torn swim suits and bleeding slices in our behinds!

Given all that, the week-long spring camping trips still were the great community building event of each year. Staff and students alike—often, particularly with those students with whom we may have had difficulty during the school year—surprisingly rising to the occasion, showing us skills, caring, and sensitivity we knew they had, but never saw. Each person returned from the Spring Camping Trips with a knapsack of memories and things learned unique to their time and place.

*****

In 1993, I was asked by Gregory Smith—then Assistant Professor in the Department of Education at Lewis and Clark College—to write a chapter about the Alternative Community School for a book he was editing, *Public Schools That Work: Creating Community*. I began that chapter, "Building Community in an Alternative Secondary School," with the following paragraph:

> "In and through community lies the salvation of the world." Thus psychologist M. Scott Peck begins the introduction to his book, *The Different Drum: Community Making and Peace* (1989). This may be overstated, yet building community is increasingly becoming a major concern in all kinds of groups from business and industry to social agencies and schools. Our need for community seems to be a basic component of who we are as human beings. Something in us yearns for connectedness to others and the transcendence of loneliness and separation. As McLaughlin and Davidson note in *Builders of the Dawn: Community Lifestyles in a Changing World*

> (1986), "The word community contains the word
> unity and, on the deepest level, community is the
> experience of unity or oneness with all people and with
> all life."

It is in this spirit, this deep sense of belonging to a genuine caring community, built through personal relationships, that the word democracy, and being a democratically-run school, is meant. As a school, this means everyone has a voice, and a vote, from the newest sixth grader to the oldest high schooler, from the most recently hired Teaching Assistant to the most experienced Teacher, and the Principal.

The overwhelming majority of the staff of the "New Junior High Program" in 1974-75 were new to what was being called "alternative education" throughout the country in the '60s and '70s, but were committed to doing school differently; making it student-centered and democratically run. Each Monday afternoon we held the democratically-run "All School Meeting" (ASM) attended by all staff and students, and facilitated by a student or students with a student note-taker, all of whom were members of the student "Agenda Committee." Staff and students submitted to the Agenda Committee items in advance that they wanted addressed by the ASM, forming the Agenda for each meeting. Decisions were typically made by consensus unless there was substantial disagreement, in which case the issue was postponed a week while those in disagreement met with a facilitator to find common ground to bring back the issue to the ASM. In some instances where time was a key factor, a 2/3 or simple majority vote was used, although this rarely occurred during my 30 year tenure. It took the staff and students time, patience, and a commitment to learn how to run a school democratically since most had no experience in democratic decision making and group processes. Although with some modifications, now some 43 years later, staff still meet weekly, or sometimes biweekly, and ASMs are typically now on Wednesdays, and sometimes bi-weekly.

There are five key components involved in what the Lehman Alternative Community School means by "democracy" in building a "democratically-run" school community:

1. Democratically-run weekly staff meetings (these are planned by a volunteer staff "Agenda Committee," and I was not a member);
2. Student and staff democratically-run weekly All School Meetings;
3. Student direct involvement in Committees,
4. Student participation in Family Groups; and
5. Spring Trips.

Our school day typically includes six 50-minute periods four times per week (some meet all five days), with two periods for a key way in which students help directly in running the school democratically—student "committees." The weekly schedule typically looks like the two grids on page 56, one for the first three, 9-week cycles, and another for the 4th cycle when students meet in their Spring Trips groups during Project times which are moved to Thursdays.

There are committees for everything from "School Maintenance," "School Modification," "Café," and "Library," to "Fibers Fundraising," "Green Thumb," "Helping Hands," and "Mediation," including the "Site-Based Council Committee" which is at the heart of the running of LACS. It runs the evaluation of courses and learning activities, and is the connection between the school and the larger "Site-Based Council" that meets once a month and includes students, staff, parents/caregivers and community members. It advises the council and provides them with information. Some years there have been grant monies available to the LACS community

Cycles 1, 2, and 3

	Monday	Tuesday	Wednesday	Thursday	Friday
9:05-9:50	Period 1			Thurs Project 1	Period 1
9:55-10:40	Period 2				Period 2
10:50-11:35	Period 3			Thurs Project 2	Period 3
11:40-12:25	Period 4				Period 4
12:25-1:05	Lunch (Period 5)				
1:05-1:45	Fam Group	Tues Proj 1	Committee	Committee	Fam Group
1:50-2:35	Period 7		Period 7		
2:40-3:25	Period 8	Tues Proj 2	Period 8		

Cycle 4

	Monday	Tuesday	Wednesday	Thursday	Friday
9:05-9:50	Period 1			Morning Project(s) and Spring Trips	Period 1
9:55-10:40	Period 2				Period 2
10:50-11:35	Period 3				Period 3
11:40-12:25	Period 4				Period 4
12:25-1:05	Lunch (Period 5)				
1:05-1:45	Fam Group	Committee	Committee		Fam Group
1:50-2:35	Period 7			Spring Trips	Period 7
2:40-3:25	Period 8				Period 8

(as from the Atlantic Philanthropic Foundation) and this Committee has gathered applications and recommended how to distribute these funds.

Community Service has been a significant part of LACS from the first year of the New Junior High Program (NJHP). That first year—as initially defined by the "Lavender Proposal"—the school year was to be divided into seven, 5-week sessions essentially of mini-courses with a day in between each of these for staff to plan the next week's classes. For the first several such sessions, the day in between was used in part to have students, in their Family Groups, do a variety of community service projects of their choosing, e.g. volunteering to help shelf books at the Tompkins County Library, to do clean up on fraternity grounds at Cornell University, assist in classrooms in one of the local elementary schools, and to clean up the beach front on a section of Cayuga Lake. In subsequent years rather than seven, 5-week sessions, we organized the academic year into five, 7-week "cycles,"[1] and when we expanded to include the high school component, we went to four, 9-week cycles to match the typical two semester (4 "quarters") high school schedule. The All School Meeting (ASM) also approved a student initiated proposal to add 30-hours of "community service" as a high school graduation requirement (approximately the number of hours in a typical 50-minute class which meets four times a week each quarter). Subsequently this requirement was amended at an ASM to double the requirement to 60-hours of community service required for graduation. Students began volunteering in a local soup kitchen helping to feed the homeless, tutoring early elementary school students, assisting in a bike repair shop

---

1.   We used the term "cycles" because we began all of our courses with a description of where we were headed, and what we wanted to learn, then at the end of the course, we would "cycle" back to see if we had accomplished our intended learning.

being run by our local Youth Bureau, and even assisting our Custodian with school maintenance

As noted in the introduction to this chapter, the Spring Camping Trip began as an "All School" event because we only had 65 students that first year. But once we grew to over 100, we had to divide into a number of smaller "Spring Trips." These experiential, week-long, alternative learning activities now continue to include not only the original tent-camping trip, but also other trips, e.g. rock climbing, wilderness camping, canoeing/camping, cross-country biking/camping, horseback-riding/camping, hiking/camping, fishing/camping, and trips with a service component, such as the Katrina relief trip to New Orleans, helping/working/camping at the "Freedom School" of the Akwesasne Mohawk Indian Reservation, traveling to foreign countries like Mexico, the Virgin Islands, Paris, and Quebec, Canada. These "Spring Trip" groups meet weekly for at least one whole afternoon for an entire 9-week quarter, planning for their trip, raising funds (beginning with what has become the annual "Fall Spaghetti Dinner" and selling of pecans fund raisers), and learning how to canoe, perform bicycle maintenance, and get in shape for those trips with the physical challenges, as well as cooking their own meals and eating together. These Trips all have common goals, such as tent-camping and living close to the earth for the week, learning to work together as a small community, meeting a physical or other personal challenge, engaging in a service component, being immersed in a foreign language and culture, and having fun! Year in and year out these trips have resulted in powerful and personally transforming experiences for our students as well as staff. There are many examples of students, and staff, who never thought they could do what was called for, who perhaps lacked the personal confidence, and yet, with the support of the group, pulled through and rose to new levels of personal strength and understanding. There is something particularly significant about being on the road, or a trail, for a week with a physical challenge, like riding a bicycle with 30-40 pounds of personal gear and a tent for 50-80 miles a day, where you only have your companions to depend on for whatever happens. It calls on the deepest of personal strengths and the highest of human qualities. These trips level the playing field, and generate respect for one another by offering the ability to see one another—students and staff—as individuals.

The LACS Belief Statements also continue to be foundational in the operation of LACS, and there are numerous illustrations of each which drive the teaching and learning. One example, The Youth Farm Project, is an outgrowth of the following four belief statements recently voted-in by the All School Meeting:

> As a democratic community, we believe that the decisions and activities of LACS should attempt to align themselves with the health of the members of the community and its environment.

> 10. In keeping with this, we believe that efforts should be made to reuse, recycle, and compost materials used on site to the best of our ability.

> 12. Also, we believe that the purchases made to keep our school running should be made locally where possible and with an attempt to minimize any negative environmental impact.

> 13. Further, we believe that the food made available at LACS should reflect an awareness of its nutritional value and its influence on the nutritional health of those who eat it.

> 14. Finally, we believe that we should make efforts to use the energy that we consume efficiently and work toward increasing our use of renewable energy sources.

Here, too, like the philosophy statements, the LACS goals have been instrumental in the development and continual modification of the curriculum by the LACS staff and students. For example, referring to belief statement #12—"To teach non-violent conflict resolution" and drawing on this quote from the Holocaust Museum—"Thou shalt not be a victim. Thou shalt not be a perpetrator. Above all, thou shalt not be a bystander."—the "WAM" program (Welcoming Allies and Mentors) was begun by students working with our social worker, with a dual mission: One, to provide new students with a mentor who will form a friendship, provide support and education, and ease the new student's transition to LACS. And two, to train the mentors and the mentees how to be helpful bystanders in situations of bias, harassment, or bullying. Each year a Core Team of students (10-12) become the task group with the responsibility to review surveys, make programmatic changes based on feedback, and design and implement the training of new mentors and orientation of new students. The following year they are responsible for the weekly teaching and training of the new mentors as well as providing mini courses for new students. The plan for WAM is to make it sustainable so that students will increasingly take ownership for planning, development and implementation of the program from year to year. Students volunteer to become WAM mentors and receive community service credit.

LACS has been a member (actually one of the original 50 schools to be granted membership) of the Coalition of Essential Schools since the founding of the Coalition by Ted Sizer of Brown University. The Coalition was founded on the following original set of nine "Common Principles:"

1. Learning to use one's mind well: The school should focus on helping young people learn to use their minds well. Schools should not be "comprehensive" if such

a claim is made at the expense of the school's central intellectual purpose.

2. Less is more, depth over coverage: The school's goals should be simple: that each student master a limited number of essential skills and areas of knowledge. While these skills and areas will, to varying degrees, reflect the traditional academic disciplines, the program's design should be shaped by the intellectual and imaginative powers and competencies that the students need, rather than by "subjects" as conventionally defined. The aphorism "less is more" should dominate: curricular decisions should be guided by the aim of thorough student mastery and achievement rather than by an effort to merely cover content.

3. Goals apply to all students: The school's goals should apply to all students, while the means to these goals will vary as those students themselves vary. School practice should be tailor-made to meet the needs of every group or class of students.

4. Personalization: Teaching and learning should be personalized to the maximum feasible extent. Efforts should be directed toward a goal that no teacher have direct responsibility for more than 80 students in the high school and middle school and no more than 20 in the elementary school. To capitalize on this personalization, decisions about the details of the course of study, the use of students' and teachers' time and the choice of teaching materials and specific pedagogies must be unreservedly placed in the hands of the principal and staff.

5. Student-as-worker, teacher-as-coach: The governing practical metaphor of the school should be student-as-worker, rather than the more familiar metaphor

of "teacher as deliverer of instructional services." Accordingly, a prominent pedagogy will be coaching, to provoke students to learn how to learn and thus to teach themselves.

6. Demonstration of mastery: Teaching and learning should be documented and assessed with tools based on student performance of real tasks. Students not yet at appropriate levels of competence should be provided intensive support and resources to assist them quickly to meet those standards. Multiple forms of evidence, ranging from ongoing observation of the learner to completion of specific projects, should be used to better understand the learner's strengths and needs, and to plan for further assistance. Students should have opportunities to exhibit their expertise before family and community. The diploma should be awarded upon a successful final demonstration of mastery for graduation—an "Exhibition." As the diploma is awarded when earned, the school's program proceeds with no strict age grading and with no system of credits earned by "time spent" in class. The emphasis is on the students' demonstration that they can do important things.

7. A tone of decency and trust: The tone of the school should explicitly and self-consciously stress values of unanxious expectation ("I won't threaten you but I expect much of you"), of trust (until abused) and of decency (the values of fairness, generosity and tolerance). Incentives appropriate to the school's particular students and teachers should be emphasized. Parents should be key collaborators and vital members of the school community.

8. Commitment to the entire school: The principal and teachers should perceive themselves as generalists

first (teachers and scholars in general education) and specialists second (experts in but one particular discipline). Staff should expect multiple obligations (teacher, counselor, manager) and a sense of commitment to the entire school.

9. Resources dedicated to teaching and learning: Ultimate administrative and budget targets should include student loads that promote personalization, substantial time for collective planning by teachers, competitive salaries for staff, and an ultimate per pupil cost not to exceed that at traditional schools by more than ten percent. To accomplish this, administrative plans may have to show the phased reduction or elimination of some services now provided students in many traditional schools.

It was after more than a year of discussion, in 1997, that the 100 members of the Coalition's governing Congress adopted the following 10th Common Principle of "Democracy and Equity:"

> The school should demonstrate non-discriminatory and inclusive policies, practices, and pedagogies. It should model democratic practices, and pedagogies. It should model democratic practices that involve all who are directly affected by the school. The school should honor diversity and build on the strength of its communities, deliberately and explicitly challenging all forms of inequity.

At LACS there currently are three student committees as described in the *Student Footbook*, in addition to WAM, that are actually led by students, with a staff support person, devoted to implementing the 10th Common Principle:

1. Students of Color and Their Allies Committee (#BlackLivesMatter): This is a space for students of color within the LACS community to come together and support one another. It is also a space for white students who are deeply committed to learning about and being a white ally. The committee is student led with staff support and can take the form of dialogue, storytelling, activism, book club, art, education, social justice awareness, community guest speakers, all school panels. Please join us and together we will continue to develop a more equitable and safe school for all students.

2. Gender and Sexual Minorities and Allies (GSMA) Committee: The mission of the LACS GSMA committee is: a) to create a safe, respectful space/community for gender and sexual minorities and their allies to be themselves, get to know each other, and create trusting and supportive relationships, b) to build group expertise on GSM history, politics, cultures and current issues, and c) to engage in outreach and activist projects to create more safety for GSM youth in our school and wider communities, and spread awareness of GSMA youth issues. For this group to be a safe space, which is a legal right protected for LGBTQ young people in the State of New York, this committee may have higher expectations of its members, and requires a group committed to this mission. It is critical to our work that it is created and carried out by volunteers (people who want to be here). Our committee welcomes people of all genders and sexual orientations who are committed to this mission.

3. Inclusive Feminists Changing Society (IFCS): "A Feminist: a person who believes in the social, economic, and political equality of the sexes." (Chimamanda

Ngozi Adiche) In this committee, we will discuss what feminism is and what it means to be a feminist in our local community, in our country, and in the world. Together we will generate ideas for activities in and out of school that will promote feminism.

Additionally, there is this student group:

The Alternative Community Court, devoted to "restorative justice" where students on both/all sides of an issue are asked what they have been thinking since the event occurred and what they think needs to happen to make things right;

And a particularly significant staff group:

The Staff "A-Team," confidentially dealing with issues of bias, and bullying.

Thus, whenever a proposal is before the All School Meeting, it first goes to the first four student committees to approve it, add an amendment, or disagree with it, thereby insuring that decisions made by a majority do not negatively impact these numerically minority groups of students. These structures and processes provide a process to help students and staff deal effectively with any incidents of racist, sexist, homophobic, and/or xenophobic harassment and intimidation.

Lastly, as Principal I also taught, and learned a great deal in the process—typically one course each nine week cycle—and most years I was the staff person working with the "Site-Based Council Committee" (described above). I particularly enjoyed working with the seniors on their "Team Interdisciplinary Projects," and teaching the high school "World Religions" course. Initially we used Huston Smith's paperback, *The*

Religions of Man, but later used his newer edition, now called *The World's Religions* (revised to be more "gender inclusive" and including a new chapter on "The Primal Religions") in the fall of 2011 and "9/11" when the airplanes crashed into the twin towers in New York City. We began the course that fall with the following "essential question" (ever since joining the Coalition of Essential Schools the staff tried to begin each class with an "essential question" as the driver of the inquiry involved in the course): "How can members of a given religion kill other people in the name of their religion/God?" To differentiate my teaching I also used an illustrated version of *The World's Religions* for some students, and a simpler paperback, *The Usborne Book of World Religions*, for those students with reading disabilities. I also used Huston Smith's initial set of eight audio tapes, "The Religions of the World" (which later became a set of five video tapes), a Bill Moyers Special, "The Wisdom of Faith," as well as another set of audio tapes, "Applied Wisdom," recorded live at an Omega Institute workshop/retreat which I attended.

The other high school course I loved developing—and students seemed to like as they requested it to be continued—was "Current Brain Research," as it allowed me to delve deeply into my strong interest in neuroscience (no doubt sparked initially by my concussions as a young man). Here I experimented with a more inductive approach, seeking to discover, with the students, what regions of the brain might be involved with different kinds of human behaviors, particularly those that involved some kind of illness such as autism, schizophrenia, phantom limb, and Tourette's syndrome. I used a series of PBS videos on "The Brain: Mind and Behavior," as well as readings of chapters from such books of Oliver Sacks' as *The Man Who Mistook His Wife for A Hat and Other Clinical Tales*, and the movie versions of his book *Awakenings* and "Rainman" with Dustin Hoffman. I learned to use videos, not in their entirety in one showing, but showing short clips from about five to 15 minutes, followed by small group and whole class discussions to extract key points and raise further questions. These were then all summarized and recorded on large newsprint using columns for: a) the region(s) of the brain possibly involved, b) the evidence, c) the source(s) of that evidence, and d) further questions raised. The "final paper/exam" for the course was a "concept map" in which students chose a part of the human body and traced the involvement and connections with the key region(s) of the brain.

There were two other high school courses that I taught which are great examples of the development of what I call our "responsive curriculum." These were two courses that were quickly inserted into the schedule for second semester courses based on key events happening in the world. The first was called "Global Environmental Health" and was in response to news from the scientific community about major issues impacting the environment. A math/computer teacher and I designed—with the students—the course for second semester 1988-89. One of our main "texts" was the December 1988 issue of *National Geographic* magazine which had an actual hologram on the cover of a crystal ball planet earth that shattered when hit by a bullet when you rotated the magazine, making the point that unless we humans change our ways, the result will be just as shattering. The first day, with an over-flowing room of students, we began with me playing the role of Mister Rogers (the children's TV show host) reading *Bartholomew and the Oobleck* with overhead projections of illustrations from the book [I'll let you readers check-out the book and make the connection if you're not already familiar with the story involving the dastardly magicians!]. After looking into and listing the various current environmental issues—ozone holes, the greenhouse effect, global warming, solid waste disposal, pesticide poisoning, extinct species, and acid rain—

the students formed teams of four and began researching their chosen topic. Periodically they reported their findings to, and received suggestions for further research from, the rest of the class, with the "final" for the course being a letter written by each team to our congress-people explaining the problem and soliciting their assistance in working on a solution.

The other example of our "responsive curriculum" was another second semester course team taught two years later dealing with the "Persian Gulf War." As many of you will recall, in mid-January of 1991 the U.S. military, with a handful of allies, invaded Iraq, and in just 42 days defeated Sadam Hussein and his army in what was known as "Operation Desert Storm." This team-taught class involved myself and two of our Social Studies teachers, working with a large group of high school students. We designed the course with an interdisciplinary approach involving science, social studies and health issues, and again divided the large class into smaller groups each researching different aspects of the Persian Gulf War and the aftermath. One of the social studies teachers worked with several groups of students to analyze how the media—different television and radio stations, newspapers, and magazines—covered the emerging war, presenting their findings in large pie charts. Like in the Global Environmental Health course, student interest was high, again illustrating the value of designing as much of the actual curriculum as possible around issues of interest to students dealing with current things happening in their world that effect them.

I also continued occasionally to teach a middle school course, such as "Middle School Health" or "Current Events," when we were short a staff person to fill a particular curricular slot in the schedule. When I taught the latter course, it resulted in the students researching and "publishing" another one of our Ox Prints, *Youth Speak*. I taught this class twice—it was, and still is a requirement that eighth graders write an original research paper. The first time, the subtitle of the Ox Print was simply *A Magazine for Young People By Young People*, and it was distributed to all the teachers, some district teachers and administrators, and extra copies for our middle school English Teachers to use with their classes. It included three "Feature" stories, three "Science" articles, two pieces of "Art and Literature," and one article in a section on "Hobbies and Recreation." The second issue included a slightly different theme in the subtitle—*A Multicultural Magazine for Young People by Young People*. The students said in the "Editorial" in the beginning of the publication why we chose that theme:

"It's really good for people to find out about other people... Maybe someday if everybody knew about each other we could live in harmony;" and "...there are 'multi-cultural people here at ACS, and all over the world. To understand the world, you have to understand the people that live on it first;" and "It helps people to be less prejudiced towards others because they understand other people's beliefs, and if they understand them it is harder to stereotype;" and "...prejudice feeds on ignorance;" and "It teaches us not to be hurt or be afraid of each other just because we're different."

This Ox Print included stories of "Human Interest," "Fashion," "Sports," "Art," "Recipes," and a center-fold-two-page-spread, "ACS Students: Where We Were Born," which included a survey done by the students of 85% of the student body at that time, with 94 born in Ithaca, 53 born elsewhere than Ithaca in New York State, 47 born elsewhere in the USA, and 22 born outside of the USA . This publication was also aimed at answering the following "essential questions:" How do we know what we know? How do we know what is true in all this news? How do we recognize bias and opinion in this news? Why does it matter if we're informed about current affairs locally, nationally, and internationally?

Thus, teaching was always a key part of each day for me as

Principal of this very special place. It not only was typically the highlight of my day, but kept me close to the heart of the school, grounded in what we were all about. So when we became a Coalition school and began designing our courses around essential questions, I was right in there struggling with my colleagues, sharing my successes and failures.

Discussion Questions

1. How will you organize the school year? Your weeks? Your days? What is your rationale?
2. Following one of the Coalition of Essential Schools main principles,"less is more," what will you include in the curriculum? What will you leave out?
3. What community resources are available in your community which can be used to supplement the things to be taught within the school?
4. What Committees would be needed to run your school?
5. Will you have "All School Meetings?" If so, what can this body decide?
6. How will you organize the staff? What leadership roles will be needed?
7. Will your Principal also teach at least one course? Why or why not?

Resources

Native American and Indigenous Peoples: Below are a few of the resources I used in teaching the "Native Religions" course as well as background for our work with the Akwesasne Reservation, and which I subsequently have found useful as

I've continued my interest in Native American and Indigenous Peoples. What Native Peoples are in your area? How will your school relate to them?

- The Iroquois (including Akwesasne Mohawks) – *The Iroquois and the Founding of the American Nation* by Donald Grinde Jr., Indian Historical Press, 1977
- *Forgotten Founders: Benjamin Franklin, the Iroquois and the Rationale for the American Revolution* by Bruce Johansen, Gambit Incorporated Publishers, 1982
- *Grandmothers Counsel the World: Women Elders Offer Their Wisdom for Our Planet*, edited by Carol Schaefer, Trumpter Boston, 2006
- DVD – "For the Next 7 Generations: 13 Indigenous Grandmothers Weaving a World That Works" – The Center for Sacred Studies Beyond Words Publishing, 2009
- *Recovering the Sacred: The Power of Naming and Claiming* by Winona LaDuke, South End Press, 2005
- *Indigenous Educational Models for Contemporary Practice: In Our Mother's Voice, Volume II*, edited by Maenetter Kape'ahiokalani Padeken Ah Nee-Benham (Michigan State University), Routledge, 2008
- *The Legal Universe: Observations on the Foundations of American Law* by Vine Deloria Jr. and David Wilkens, Fulgrum Publishing, 2011
- *The Elder Brothers: A Lost South American People and Their Message about the Fate of the Earth* by Alan Ereira, Alfred Knoph Publishers, 1992
- DVD – "Aluna: There is no Life without thought," FilmRise, 2012
- *Light at the Edge of the World: A Journey Through the Realm of Vanishing Cultures*, Douglas and McIntyre, 2007

- *The Wayfinders: Why Ancient Wisdom Matters in the Modern World*, House of Anansi Press, 2009, and the DVD by the same title from San Simeon Films, 2010 – all by Wade Davis (anthropologist, ethnobotanist, filmmaker, photographer, author, and National Geographic Explorer-in-Residence)
- *Braiding Sweetgrass: Indigenous Wisdom, Scientific Knowledge and the Teachings of Plants* by Robin Wall Kimmerer, 2013, published by Milkweed Editions, Minneapolis, Minnesota

Chapter Four

Family Group
An Essential Ingredient

❝ *If full participation of our students in our democratic self-governance is the 'backbone' of [L]ACS, then clearly Family group is the 'heart' of [L]ACS.*"[1]

In a paper, written in March of 1976 in the 2nd semester of our 2nd year, by our original math teacher (now a lawyer in New York City) entitled "Leading a Family Group in an Alternative Junior High: A Log," he noted:

> The staff agreed before the school began that each student should be assigned to a staff member, who would act in a teacher-counselor role. Thus each staff person chose five to ten students and "Teacher-Counselor (T-C) Groups" were formed. These met ten minutes every day for attendance and announcement purposes. Also each Teacher-Counselor dealt with the discipline, credits and scheduling of his/her counselees.
>
> As the first year progressed, the students and staff increasingly felt a need for small discussion groups to process school decisions. The All School Meeting format was too unwieldy and many people had

1.   From an article I wrote entitled "Family Groups at Ithaca's Alternative Community School" for the Summer 1986 issue of the *National Coalition News* of the National Coalition of Alternative Community Schools (NCACS).

difficulties in expressing themselves in large groups. These discussion groups were formed by peer relations. People soon came to realize that we did not really need a discussion group different from the T-C group. With a minimum of reorganization students could choose the staff person with whom they wanted to work and the T-C group could serve both functions. Two periods a week were set aside for these group meetings.

Meanwhile many groups had been regularly eating dinners together, going bowling, going to movies and generally had begun developing in action oriented ways.

Many staff members were beginning to feel uncomfortable and incompetent as Teacher-Counselors. No one set aside the time to plan or to structure the groups; and the staff never met to discuss the educational framework of the T-C groups. Each group grew independently of every other.

As the staff discussed these problems, they agreed that a priority for the second year would be to integrate the T-C group into the educational direction of the school. A workshop was set up for August [see the following brainstormed list of things to do in Family Group formed in this workshop, as well as ideas from a follow-up workshop done the next year].

During the workshop, through role playing and lengthy discussions, a focus of support groups was found for the T-C groups. The emphasis was changed from a staff to a peer group orientation, by simply changing the selection procedure. Instead of having staff members choose students or having students pick staff members, the students would be asked to group themselves together with friends. Thus, first the group would form and then a staff person would be chosen as the leader by the students. To emphasize its distinction from the T-C groups, the newly defined groups were called Family Groups.

The Family Group had many varied functions [see the current list which will follow]: support, peer relationships, the discipline of its members, the discussion of school business, scheduling, evaluations [written "report cards"], and credits. The Family Group Leader was responsible for keeping track of all of this as well as doing individual counseling, contacting parents, and educating the students in group skills.

In an article I wrote for the Coalition News (initial publication of the Coalition of Essential Schools) I described the following ten (10) functions of Family Groups, which have remained primarily the same today at LACS:

1. Counseling: This happens on a formal and informal basis, in individual and group situations. The counseling may involve personal as well as school issues. It may happen during and after school. This type of relationship between student and staff member lends permanence and credibility, as well as personal closeness, to the daily working relationship between students and teachers and gives the Family Group leader a greater knowledge of the whole student and his/her life situation in and out of school. This allows for better program planning and implementation for students on an individual basis. When a student has difficulty in following the program s/he has chosen, it is the responsibility of the Family Group Leader, occasionally with the help of the Support Team to set up an accountability system which will provide the external controls and/or motivation to help that

student in following his/her program for a short period until they are able again to function more independently.

2. Administrative/Program Planning: This includes filling out various school district forms, distributing information, and discussing upcoming events. Another major function of Family Groups is program planning, i.e. the filling out of students' schedules for each of the nine-week cycles of our school calendar. This planning is a process of communication between parents/caregivers, staff and Family Group leader. The Family Group leader also has the responsibility for monitoring the progress of a student's program, and for discussing teachers' evaluations with students and parents/caregivers.

3. Parent/Caregiver School Communication and Community-building: The Family Group, through the leader, is the funnel for school-home communication. Notice of school events is often passed on to students in Family Groups, to be passed-on to home. Informal evening meetings of Family Group parents/caregivers may be held periodically, in the home of parents/caregivers and serve as a way for them to share their perceptions and experiences of school and their children, to ask questions of staff, and to discuss among themselves school issues. The Family Group leader is the first point of contact for these concerns and questions.

4. Friendship and Social/Peer Identity: Family Group is a place to form new friendships, strengthen old ones, and discuss what friendship means. It is a place for friends to gather to do things other than "hang-out" and gossip. Thus, Family Group allows youngsters to learn about themselves in social settings, in task-

oriented situations, and in decision-making situations. A student has the opportunity to try out different aspects of self in a relatively non-threatening situation.

5. Social Skills/Group Building: In Family Groups, students begin to learn to work with others in organized group settings to develop skills required in social situations, and to learn those qualities of a group which make it successful and functional. To this end, special Inservice Workshops are held periodically for Family Group leaders to improve their own skills in group processes.

6. Group Skills/Interaction: Students participate fully in the decision-making at LACS. Much of this discussion and decision-making goes on in Family Groups. They often are presented with problems about which they are asked for opinions and solutions which they would be willing to carry out. Students have a chance to learn the process of decision-making and how they as individuals fit into that process as a genuine "laboratory in democracy" or citizen education. Thus, students come to have more ownership of the problems and solutions which confront them and the school. Students are encouraged to take leadership for/ of the group, and this is enhanced by the skills learned in Family Group.

7. Developing a Consciousness of Alternative Education: Many of the concepts, activities and tasks which make LACS "alternative" are centered around Family Groups. Scheduling and choosing classes, decision-making, and counseling all take place during Family Group time each week. Family Group is also the place to discuss issues which confront us as an alternative school, and affect the students. The closing of our original building and our relocation, the creation of

our alternative high school component, the issues of joint occupancy with Ithaca High School, and the process of district-wide reorganization have all been topics of discussion at Family Groups.

8. Recreational: Family Groups often engage in recreational activities. This not only involves having fun, but also developing, planning, and organizing skills of both individuals and the group as a whole. It also allows students to be with each other in situations other than classwork. It enables the Family Group leader to relate to students in other than the Teacher-Counselor role, and to learn about each student in unique situations.

9. Check-In: The Family Group is the means for regular check-ups with respect to how students are doing. It is done by going around the group simply asking each student to say how they are doing. If the Family Group leader senses that there is a significant mental or physical health issue which needs attention, then s/he is expected to contact the appropriate Support Team staff (Guidance Counselor, Nurse, Social Worker, Psychologist)

10. Discipline/Conflict Resolution: The discipline process at LACS begins with the Family Group and Family Group leader; if a satisfactory solution cannot be worked out, the problem proceeds to the student Alternative Community Court (now the Restorative Justice Council), which is composed of a student representative from each Family Group. Thus the Family Group has major responsibility for affecting student behavior in school. Often, rather than "discipline" per se, Family Group leaders work with their students to resolve conflict through techniques of "dispute resolution and third-party intervention"

conferences. And to this end, the staff is engaged periodically in Inservice Training.

Family Groups have been formed both in the first few days of each school year, or in the end of the previous school year with new students added subsequently. Students are expected to stay with the Family Group to which they are assigned at least for the first month of the school year, after which they may ask for a switch. This request must be honored both by the Family Group Leader from whose Group they wish to leave, and the Family Group they wish to join. The following is an overview of the "Family Group Preference Sheet" recently used in 2016-17 to form Family Groups, beginning with this from the Introduction:

> Family Group is a key part of the LACS curriculum. The main goal of Family Group [see GBE Essential 1A] is to demonstrate that you can "work and live cooperatively with others." These others may or may not be your friends when you join the Group. The goal challenges each group member to learn to work effectively together. A Family Group trip is a major commitment. If you choose one, make sure that you fully understand what is expected of you. Ask the trip leader(s) before you sign up if you are not sure of the commitment. Switching out of a trip group can be particularly disruptive to the group. Family Groups are formed by members of the support staff who do their absolute best to keep your preferences in mind. However, there are 300 students who each have preferences, and it is simply not always possible to honor everyone's first choice.

There are four sections to the "Preference Sheet" which

begins with blanks for the student's name and grade level. [Note that several have a service or personal challenge component]:

A) Students are asked to check one option in each of these pairs indicating what is most important to them:
   I. ( ) Staff Family Group Leader – or – ( ) Students in your Family Group
   II. ( ) Focused Family Group – or – ( ) Regular Family Group
   [Note - as you will see below, a "Focused Group" is one that will be doing an activity together throughout the year and during Spring Trips week]
B) Students are directed to "number in the order of your preference" any of the list of Focus Family Groups, the following are some of them for 2016-17:
   • For Middle Schoolers only, Crafty Crew with the following description: "If you'd like your focus to be on crafting, this Family Group will be a perfect fit! We will work as a group to innovate and share ideas, techniques, and supplies."
   • For Middle or High Schoolers, Bike Group: "If you are a bike rider at any level, or, are interested in becoming one please sign up for this focused Family Group. We will plan occasional fall and spring weekend rides together and learn about basic bike maintenance like fixing broken chains and patching tires."
   • For 8th-10th graders only, International Permaculture and Reforestation: "Are you someone who cares about the planet, likes to help others and wants to work hard so we can make a difference somewhere in the world?"
   [The following are all for High School students only]

- Community Service: "This Family Group will be perfect for students who would like to get involved in Community Service. In addition to the normal fun activities, such as fundraiser dances, sleepovers, movies, etc. we will spend one day a week for 20 weeks or more, helping out at "Loaves and Fishes" during lunch [a local agency that provides meals for the homeless]."
- Localvores: "Localvores" will be redefining itself as a group in some pretty cool ways. We will continue to spend time bringing fresh local produce into the meals served at school, but will also put fresh energy into a few other interesting projects. One will be re-designing the cafeteria space—thinking about beautiful wall hangings, music, plants, etc. Another will be our connection to the Youth Farm through pop-up from markets at school and making pesto and jam for sale. Finally, we'll work toward some sort of fun 'lunch menu addition' at least a couple of times each nine-week cycle—planning and making things like sushi and summer rolls."
- Katrina Relief: "Want to make a difference to people who are trying to put their lives back together after experiencing/living through a natural disaster? The people of New Orleans are still rebuilding. This Family Group will spend our time learning about how we can help make a difference. We will establish connections with the New Orleans community and we will fundraise to contribute to the relief efforts and to cover expenses so we can go and be of service during trips week."

- Service/Akwesasne Freedom School: "This Family Group will focus on getting involved in the Ithaca community—and beyond—through service. We will complete over 100 hours of service through both individual placements and group projects that we design. We will explore ideas and service and community, and, as a group, decide where and how we want to help out around Ithaca. The Family Group course [it will meet 4 times per week as a high school class] will be linked to the Mohawk Trip in May. We will also study Native American cultures (mainly Haudenosaunee) and raise awareness about the Freedom School—the school we visit in the Akwesasne Mohawk Nation."

- Spanish Language Immersion: "Members of this group commit to working together all year raising awareness and funds to travel to the Instituto Linguistico Francisco Marroquin in Antigua, Guatemala or other destinations with similar opportunities.... All participating students must be enrolled in or involved with a Spanish class during the trip year either at LACS or an approved equivalent."

C) "Regular" Family Groups: [those without a specific focus or theme—this is a list of the 18 LACS staff who will be Family Group leaders for the 2016-17 school year] "If Family Group leader is important to you, give several options that would make you feel happy. Those staff names marked with an * are those who have proposed to lead a "Focused Family Group." If there are not enough students who sign up for their "Focused Family Group," then these staff will have a "regular" Family Group. Feel free to check the leaders you would like to have even if you are not interested in their Focus Group."

D) "Write the names of students you would like to get to know in Family Group. You may list as many as you wish; please list at least three. The more students you list, the greater the possibility of being with one of them."

*****

Since a key component of Family Groups is learning to live and work together as a group, the following summary of group process is taken from staff development workshops done early in our history, *Notes for Family Group Leaders on Group Development*[2]—*Stages of Group Development—An Overview*:

Clearly, no two groups are alike. Each is a unique creation of the adjustment to, and the interactions of, its individual members, each of whom comes from his or her own unique life space, with differing life perspectives, experiences, coping mechanisms, goals, and methods of relating to the world.

Despite the presenting uniqueness of each group, throughout the life of any group, it proceeds through a basic, general developmental sequence. Numerous authors have presented models of group development and identified a sequence of specific stages in the life of any group. It is vital for the leader to have a basic understanding of how a group functions, how it grows, and what may be expected at given points. The purpose in offering a model is to provide a leader with an index to more effectively assess and monitor a group's process, and to provide a framework in which it becomes easier to evaluate and select appropriate interventions.

2.   Based on material originally presented by Gale Livingston-Smith at an ACS staff workshop on 29 August 1979 with new material in "italics" from the 1993 manual *Facilitation Skills for Team Leaders* by Hackett and Martin.

A cautionary note, the following developmental stages are rarely well demarcated. There is considerable overlap and the boundaries between them are fuzzy; rarely does a group permanently graduate from one phase to another. Phases emerge, become dominant, then recede, only to have the group return again later to deal with the same issues with greater thoroughness; as in most any relationship.

A) Forming:
1. Coming together as separate individuals
2. An aggregate of strangers with little or no commitment to one another
3. No identifiable group structure or boundaries
4. Individuals utilizing comfortable dysfunctional behavior patterns as defense mechanisms to establish their own positions with the aggregate, i.e. scapegoating, challenging the purpose and integrity of the group, ridiculing one another, etc.
5. Frequently conversation revolves around "then and there" situations as an effort to establish power or position
6. Individual challenging of leader's position

"Facilitator" (Family Group Leader) Behaviors:
- Ensure (Family Group) members get acquainted
- Be sensitive to team members' needs
- Provide clear direction and information
- Give team simple tasks
- Provide intensive "awareness" training
- Provide team-building activities

B) Storming:
1. Bring about an awareness between group members of one another

2. Alliance building (factionalism) that often takes form of cliques
3. Cliques are established usually from the position of previously established delinquent patterns rather than with a view towards the reality of the present situation; old values and attitudes reaffirmed
4. Cliques do not have positive allegiance to the group as a whole; challenge very existence of the group with aggression directed toward the symbolic group leader
5. Conflict and jockeying for position between subgroups, especially over the way the group is run
6. Cliques' external boundaries often weak, allowing shifting of membership and allegiances; allows for beginning of problem solving mechanism
7) Communication process is initiated

Facilitator Behaviors:
- Continue to be positive and informative
- Reassure Family Group that current conflict is normal
- Deal openly with conflict
- Give Family Group more responsible tasks
- Continue to use team-building activities

C) Norming:
1. Extremely important stage; ways of behaving within the group and the school community as a whole are examined and discussed and definite behavior being established as acceptable or unacceptable
2. "Rules" of conduct for the Family Group are

formulated to regulate the internal boundaries and proactive behaviors

3. Relationship of cliques to the whole group and its well-being are examined resulting in the breakdown of the factions and formulation of cohesion among the members

4. Old values and attitudes of individual members are explored and altered to the extent that they affect the well-being of the Family Group

5. Individual members begin to recognize that with the increased level of awareness and responsibility toward other members of the Family Group their own needs are being met more expeditiously

6. Individuals recognize a commonality of problem and purpose with the Family Group, disassociate themselves from delinquent norms

Facilitator Behaviors:
- Provide less structure as Family Group matures
- Give Family Group more responsibility, e.g. members take leadership roles
- Ensure Family Group does not overly rely on any one member
- Provide Family Group development activities

D) Performing:
1. Problems, both individual and group, are actively recognized and attacked by the group as a whole

2. Well established methods for taking care of business

3. Camaraderie established with the feeling of shared ownership

4. Leader acts more in a facilitative role

5. Willingness to strive for consensus[3] rather than

problem solve by some other method, e.g. voting, authority, etc.

6. As with true intimacy, this stage is a transient one, and there are not long periods where the group can maintain itself at this level of intensity

Facilitator Behaviors:

- Ensure Family Group's information needs are fulfilled
- Ensure that the Family Group celebrates its successes
- Encourage team toward continued growth
- Ensure new members are brought in
- Reduce your involvement as Family Group grows more functional
- Continue to foster trust and commitment among team members

The following are some of the resources for Family Groups that we developed or learned about through professional

3. Consensus decision making involves reaching concordance, and is not majority rule, nor does it mean everyone has to agree. Rather it means simply that everyone "consents to" or can "buy into" a decision. To test for consensus, a Facilitator asks, "Are there any objections to the decision being proposed?" [It helps to have it written on newsprint, a chalkboard, or overhead so everyone can see it clearly.] If there are objections, they are heard, and then each person stating an objection is asked if they are: 1) willing to "stand aside" and let the decision go forward, perhaps with a trial period—or asked if they are: 2) willing to "stand aside" having expressed their concern or doubt, but agree to let the decision go forward, or asked if they want to "block" the decision and not let it go forward for a specific reason(s), which requires a revision to be made to the proposed decision before being brought back to test again for consensus. [Here a specific short time period is given for this revision to be created and typically one or two persons who liked the original proposal agree to work with the "objector" in constructing the revised proposal.] The process is then repeated with the revised proposal. If this does not produce consensus—or if the decision has a time limitation—the Facilitator may have to use a 2/3 or simple majority vote. [based on material in the paperback, *On Conflict and Consensus: A Handbook on Formal Consensus Decision Making* by C. T. Lawrence Butler and Amy Rothstein, Food Not Bombs Publishing, 2nd Edition, 1991]

development workshops. These are offered here in the hope that they may be useful to those doing, or considering doing an alternative school—*Ideas for Family Group Leaders* (from staff Family Group Leader brainstorming and workshop, January 1976):

1. Volleyball
2. Blind walk
3. How people see each other (pick an animal, a season, or ?)
4. Originator   Pawn
   /_____/_____/_____/_____/_____/_____/
   (rate yourself and others)
5. Storytelling
6. Joke telling
7. Films or seeing a movie together
8. Pool, pinball, ping-pong tournament
9. Listing goals and comparing (e.g. what Family Group means to me)
10. Various communication exercises
11. Curriculum [classes, projects] feedback/evaluation
12. Disagree   Agree
    /_____/_____/_____/_____/_____/_____/
    (each student rates an issue)
13. Fund raising for Spring Trips and/or a special Family Group event
14. Lunch and/or dinner together
15. Delegate students to Family Group roles—facilitator, resource finder, order keeper, note/record-keeper, etc.
16. Decision-making experiences—prioritize, study processes, use problem-solving methodologies
17. Getting to know each other exercises – e.g. "An important thing about me is _____?"; "Something that makes me (sad, happy, etc.)

18. Break into small groups, triads, pairs, for exercises
19. Plan group trip, or short excursion in town
20. Non-verbal exercises—high-tension wire (get everyone over), pass imaginary object, theater games
21. Hiking, fishing, bowling, ice-skating, cross-country skiing, roller-skating, skate-boarding, roller-blading

Additional Family Group Ideas (from October 1996 Mini-Workshop brainstorming on a Superintendent's Conference Day):

1. Move all tables together create more of a group feeling
2. Get off campus
3. Do something active, get out of the building!
4. Group challenge (e.g. "trust-fall," use the "wall" and three posts outside to the north of the building)
5. Fund-raising/common focus
6. Written games/silly games [see samples which follow from notebook prepared by Maggie Goldsmith]
7. Common goal for the year
8. Make a connection with each student in the Family Group; interview privately each member in beginning of the year
9. Interview the group about what they like to do
10. Pick apples at a local orchard
11. Write down 2-3 activities each individual likes to do on index cards
12. [Experienced Family Group Leaders "buddy-up" with new ones]
13. Assign tasks/jobs for each member (e.g. note-taker, attendance-taker)
14. Group challenge activities/exercises
15. Use of Cayuga Nature Center for special time off-campus

16. Solicit parents/caregivers, neighbors, friends for paid jobs as fundraisers
17. Cooperative games, e.g. partners "thumb wrestle"
18. Sometimes just do it; don't always have to have discussion and consensus!
19. Role play "good and bad" manners, particularly before going out in public!
20. "Pictionary" and other board games (Taboo, Outburst, Balderdash, etc.)
21. Focus on academics, how they can support each other, do homework
22. [Family Group Leaders—ask Support Staff for help, suggestions]
23. [Family Group Leader—participate in games with your students!]
24. Pick trash for cash (e.g. at Cornell fraternity houses after weekend parties)
25. Challenge other Family Groups to various games
26. Visit places important to each Family Group member
27. Plan a special activity/event for each Family Group member, e.g. birthdays
28. Be sure to listen to everyone, not just to main talkers
29. Older high school Family Groups do something with middle schoolers
30. Find a way to define our Family Group as special—e.g. first to raise $100, secret acts of kindness, etc.

Also from October 1996 Mini-Workshop—Some things to look for in groups:

- Participation
- Group atmosphere
- Influence
- Membership

- Styles of influence
- Norms
- Decision-making processes
- Leadership
- Task functions
- Maintenance functions
- Seating arrangement

Some things to consider in evaluating your Family Group's effectiveness:

- Attendance
- Participation
- Seriousness
- Students maintain order
- Students initiate
- Total group function
- Everybody following
- Feels good
- Support each other
- Students say its going well
- Accomplish tasks
- Even one person gets something out of it
- Students & leaders goals compatible
- Group now feels better than it did before
- Positive group spin-off
- Group has fun together

*****

The following material is a sample of activities for Family Group Leaders developed by Maggie Goldsmith[4], English/

---

4. Maggie Goldsmith passed away in October 2013.

Drama Teacher in 1997—*Games for LACS Family Groups: An Introduction*—with an example from her 2004 Supplement:

What is Family Group, anyway? We all come to it with different expectations and needs, but one of the goals is always to learn to work together. Here are games for the times when your group wants to do something together and needs a new idea, or when the group wants help focusing before a discussion.

This is just a project I put together during some free time in my sabbatical year, in February 1997. I hope your group can use some of the games through your forming, storming and norming periods—leading to the ideal stage, when you are together, performing!

Why play games? They are fun! They are relaxing. They help us see each other and ourselves in new ways. They help bring the group together. Set up ground rules. Work together to build a supportive group who depend on each other, trust each other, and work creatively with each other. Use the discussion questions at the end of each game to analyze how your group works together, to understand different members' needs, and to stimulate ideas of how your group can improve communication and support."

The games fall into three categories [a few examples have been taken from each category, and from the Supplement; the full booklet is available in the LACS library and the LACS Archives located at Cornell University].

A) Games for Group Closeness will help your Family Group come to a common focus so everyone is more primed for an important discussion or meeting. They are games you can play quickly, allowing time for Family Group business.

Active Listening

Use this game on a day when you have Family Group business to work on together but your minds are not ready, yet. It will help you come together and listen to each other. Or, use this game when people come upset to a Family Group meeting; a thoughtful discussion of a serious issue will be easier after this game.

Materials: none

Directions: Sit in pairs, face to face, close to each other. For one minute (someone can set a watch or timer) player A in each pair talks nonstop about something personally important, while player B listens actively. When the minute is over, player B restates, by telling player A what s/he has heard. Then A and B switch roles.

A Variation: After the first telling and restating, all the A players move to the left, to new B players. Then B talks while the new A listens. Last, the A player restates. Continue to shift pairs: A player always moves left and B player stays in the same place; A player will talk and B listen and restate on the odd numbered rounds, B player talks and A listens and restates on the even numbered rounds.

Active listening is saying little and encouraging the speaker to go on. Something personally important can be silly, serious, sensitive or selfish! The group or a leader can decide on specific topics ahead of time, like "Plans for the weekend." If the group is successful with these rules, try, on another day, groups of three, then four, then five.

Discussion: Is listening a skill? How about restating, is that a skill? Explain.

Lies

Lies tell us a lot about each other, just as the truth does. This game is a way to get to know each other and have some fun together, at any point in the year.

Materials: paper or 3x5 cards and pencils or pens

Directions: Sit in a circle. Each player writes on a card or piece of paper, three things about him or herself. Two will be true, one will be a lie. But they all should sound true. Take turns reading out from your card, while the group tries to guess which statement is the lie. Examples are, "My middle name is Bridgeport, " "I broke my leg when I was five," "My family has moved seven times in my life," and so forth.

Listen to each other carefully. Take a vote, if you want, when choosing the false statement. The winners are actually the ones who tell the most convincing lies

Discussion: How does a lie tell a lot about the person who tells it?

B) Games for Group Challenges require the group to work together. For these games you will need to communicate with each other and take risks together. Some of these games are perfect for the times when two Family Groups want to join for an activity that isn't "Capture the Flag," when they may want to take a challenge together or just play together.

ABC

Demonstrated by the EXIT ONLY theatre group that visited [L]ACS in 1995, this game is a challenge. It takes concentration!

Materials: none

Directions: Sit in a circle or so you can all see and hear each other. Choose any letter to start, say, for example "O." Every sentence that follows must begin with the consecutive letter of the alphabet. Listen to a story unfold as each player says the next sentence! See how long you can keep the story developing. If you get to Z go back to A.

Example, for 14 players, starting with the letter "O:"
Oh no!
Put it there!
Question, I have a question.
Right, go ahead, ask it.
So, who says it should go there?
Tim does.
Under the table?
Very funny!
Why not?
X-rays go through the table.
Yes, but the chances are still good.
Zero, I'd say.
All right, then, forget it!
But then, where can we put it?

Try to keep the pace fast. That takes some practice! Maybe four or five players want to demonstrate before the whole group tries together. Will it help to write the alphabet across the chalkboard before starting the game?

Discussion: How does this game help us develop skill in listening?

Group Juggle

You have probably played this game or some variation of it. If you do not know each other's names, this game is a challenge .... and helpful. It takes concentration and communication .... real working together. And when your Family Group is good at it, invite another Family Group to join you!

Materials: a few soft, light balls, bean bags, or rolled pairs of socks in distinct colors.

Directions: Stand in a circle [the Family Group leader can be the first player.]. One player calls out another player's name [someone not next to that player, but across the group], looking at that person, then tosses underhand a ball to that player, [note, "tosses" not throws, lobs!]. The second player tosses/lobs the ball to another, first calling out that player's name. Continue tossing the ball to new players until everyone has received and tossed the ball and it returns to the first player. Remember the pattern, the sequence. Continue to toss the ball again, calling to each other, following the pattern established in the first go-round. When the pattern and pace are clear and steady, stop using names, and add a second ball [or other object]; then add a third, then a fourth, adding as many objects as the group thinks they can juggle. Try to keep the pace steady. You can time a round and then try to beat your own record.

Discussion: When someone drops the ball, how do they feel? What should the group do when the ball is dropped?

C) Games for Group Relaxation are just fun, to help you enjoy being together, just ideas of things to do together. If one or two people do not want to join, the game can still go on.

Book "Reports"

This game encourages you to "think on your feet" and to laugh together.

Materials: a box, can, or hat and slips of paper and pencils or pens

Directions: any arrangement of the room is fine, as long as you can see and hear the speaker. First, everyone makes up and then writes (clean and not personal) fictional titles of books on the slips of paper, folds the papers, and drops them in the container. A volunteer then draws out a paper with a title, thinks for a few seconds, and then tells the story that goes with the title, that is, "reports on the book." The group listens actively but does not prompt or help. Take turns drawing titles and describing the story that might go with that title.

Examples, created by [L]ACS students:

- Growing Up as a Hamster; the Inside Story
- Doorway Back to the End
- My Life as a Lamp
- Solitude
- Shira, Princess of Power, Meets Captain America
- The Afterlife of a Condemned Man
- Trainride into Nihilism
- Deceit in Utopia
- Woodrow Wilson and Me
- The Thought that Burned
- The Case of the Missing Magnet
- Breath of the Serpent Woman

Encourage each speaker to comment on the "author's" style of writing and choice of subject. The group can time these to about two minutes, or just let the speakers go on, extemporaneously. A variation is to write one title on the chalkboard and pair up to create and write a synopsis; then take turns reading them to each other and/or the whole group.

Join a Story

You have probably told group stories before. This game invites you to tell the story by becoming a character in it and helping to set the scene.

Materials: none

Directions: Sit in a circle or so you can all see and hear each other. One player starts the story by saying, "I am ... " And describing, in a characteristic voice, a person or object in a place, telling what that character wants. Take turns around the circle, adding new characters and telling what they want. Stop after everyone has joined the story, or continue for a second round, either with the same characters or with additional ones. The last person should describe the end to the story.

Example:

- I am a baby. Here I am in the playpen, and nobody ever pays attention to me...My diaper smells, and all my toys are on the floor where I can't reach them. I want to cry!
- I am the big sister. I can't find my green sweater, and it's too cold to go out with out it—the house smells and I need some fresh air.
- I am the plant in the corner. I am covered in dust and parched for water. Why doesn't someone notice me?
- I am Grandfather. I just stopped in to get out of the freezing cold, but with two children wailing and a wilting plant in the corner, I'm not sure I should stay.
- I am the family dog, Rover. I am very happy today because I have so many things to chew on—this green sweater for instance, and then, any one of those toys lying around.

Don't worry about the character you become. The story belongs to the group, and everything adds to the story. Do try to pull in characters and points already established.

Discussion: Do you prefer to create a story in a group or alone.

*****

From the Game Book Supplement

"You're here at [L]ACS with a way to grow into our middle name ["Community"]; keep playing games together!
–Love Always, Maggie"

Up Jenkins

This game was introduced to PAL [the 6th grade "People Art and Literature" class], and takes a while to play a few sets, so plan ahead!

Materials: a quarter; line up tales end to end so teams can sit across from each other at a long table. Set chairs along both sides of the tables, one per player.

Directions: Form two teams of equal number, and sit along the table, facing the other team. One side (Team A) has the quarter and passes it or pretends to pass it hand to hand under the table. The other side (Team B) tries to follow the movement of the quarter by watching faces. Team B calls out to Team A, "Up Jenkins!" Team A then raises their fists, closed, against the table, and in unison, they count "1,2,3 Down Jenkins!" while they hit their elbows three times (1,2,3) on the table, and then in unison slap down their palms ("Down Jenkins") onto the table. The object is to cover the sound of the quarter hitting the table. Team B then taps hands of Team A to find the quarter. Each tap is one point Team B does not want! When the quarter is found, it goes to Team B to pass and pretend to pass while Team A now guesses where the quarter is.

Discussion: How does your team make choices of

which hand to tap? Is it awkward to communicate up and down a line?

Discussion Questions

1. How would you form Family Groups? By grade level? Randomly with an equal number of males and females? By interests?
2. Should students remain in their Family Group for their whole secondary school career at your school? Should/could they change each year? What are the advantages and disadvantages of each approach?
3. Should every staff member have a Family Group? Why or why not? If not, who should not have a Family Group? Some schools do not have the administrators or support team (Counselors, Social Worker, School Psychologist, Nurse, etc.) have a Family Group, what are the pros and cons?
4. How often should Family Groups meet each week? For how long?

Resources

- Family Groups: There are two publications that are helpful in creating and organizing what others call "Advisory Groups" – *The Power of Advisories: Changing Systems to Personalize Learning*, by the Education Alliance at Brown University, 2003; and *The Advisory Guide: Designing and Implementing Effective Advisory Programs in Secondary Schools*, by Rachel Poliner and Carol Miller Lieber, Educators for Social Responsibility (ESR), 2004

Chapter Five

Evaluation of Learning and Staff

*T*wo years before moving to Ithaca and starting the New Junior High Program, I had the opportunity to attend the "National Conference on Grading Alternatives" in Cleveland, Ohio. There I had my thinking about evaluating student learning turned completely around. Here are a few of my notes from The Notebook, which I mentioned in the foreword. In the opening address, "A Personal Search for a Grade," it was noted that letter grades are often "life shapers," certainly not an effective way to describe a given student's learning, and, in contrast to written evaluations, are like squeezing all the letters of the alphabet into one! In an "Overview of Grading Alternatives," the importance of students doing self-evaluations based on clearly understood objectives or expectations was noted, and everyone was reminded of the difference in formative and summative evaluation, encouraging more use of the latter. Other workshop sessions included a trio of urban educators who made the case for closing schools (meaning not holding classes) for two days to have child/parent/teacher conferences. This latter recommendation is done mid-year at LACS, and these sessions now are led by each student with written evaluations that: a) include what the learning objectives were for the course and how they were addressed, b) the teacher's written description of how the student progressed in meeting these objectives, c) if s/he "met expectations," *"exceeded expectations," or "has not yet met expectations" (note "failed" wasn't an option, and each student had the opportunity to successfully complete the expectation within a given time period and with additional help as needed), and d) the student's self-evaluation, all with specific examples.*

Our use of these kinds of written evaluations (now being done online, digitally) is still sometimes questioned, particularly by new parents/caregivers who worry about their daughter or son getting into college without ACT or SAT scores, letter grades, or a GPA (grade point average). The National Center for Fair and Open Testing, as of winter 2017, lists 925 colleges and universities who ". . . will make decisions about all or many applicants without considering ACT or SAT scores." They go on to note that"Too often, accountability has been reduced to standardized tests that measure a limited range of academic skills, thereby narrowing [the high school] curriculum and teaching." Most colleges and universities know that ACT and/or SAT scores are simply not effective predictors of students' success in college. Thus, they are more interested in what a student has done during her/his high school years, including community service, special projects, and what they say in their college application essay. Rather than hindering or handicapping LACS graduates in their college applications, they are often actively sought after by college admissions people. [See more in the Resources listed at the end of this chapter.]

*****

Graduation and promotion by exhibition came about after at least a year and a half (1987-1989) of the whole school community—students, staff, and parents/caregivers—looking to move away from the typical high school credit/Carnegie unit system, to a more authentic way for students to demonstrate their skills, knowledge, and attitudes as being developed by the Coalition of Essential Schools. This involved an extensive review process under the heading "Committee to Re-evaluate and Re-vitalize our Curriculum" or C2RC [in the spirit of the then popular characters from the "Star Wars" movies, C3PO and R2D2!]; with a series of eight sub-committees for all areas of our curriculum – science/health, social studies, English/drama, math/computers, foreign languages, physical education, fine arts (music and art), home and career skills and technology. What follows is the latest addition of the high school graduation and middle school promotion requirements taken from the *Lehman Alternative Community School Student Footbook*.[1]

LACS High School Graduation Requirements

The Essential Question: "How can you exhibit that you have the skills, knowledge, and attitudes needed to be a global citizen?" Answering the essential question requires each potential graduate to prepare and present the following final graduation exhibitions to their graduation committee in the spring of the year they intend to graduate:

1. A Team Interdisciplinary Graduation Project to be presented publicly which will:

   • Be completed in small teams of three or more seniors;
   • Involve selecting an issue or topic that will draw on the skills, knowledge, and attitudes that the students have developed throughout high school;
   • Demonstrate historical research;

1. Rather than the typical "Guidebook," this booklet provides "step-by-step" directions to all of the processes of student life at LACS!

- Use the different methodologies of critical thinking and problem solving;
- Connect concepts from two or more Essential areas;
- Be communicated in a second language, or include a critique of the intercultural impact of the project;
- Involve taking a public stand or position to be presented orally and in writing.

Some of the early "Team Interdisciplinary Graduation Projects" with which I was involved as a staff advisor included the researching, publishing, and distributing in the Ithaca Community, pamphlets or booklets on local topics. These involved: "Big-box Business and Ithaca's Economy: A Look at Ithaca's Options for Economic Development," including Ithaca Dollars, and a directory of locally owned small businesses; "No Child Left Behind: the Decline of Music and Arts in Schools," with specific proposals and programs to save these activities; and "A Guide to Genetically Modified Foods," including the scientific process of genetic modification, the ethical and political debate, and the regulatory measures in place. But it was the team that worked on "adolescent brain research" that was particularly fulfilling for me. This Team of seniors presented their research findings—that there is a phase shift in the adolescent brain driven by hormonal changes which cause adolescents to need to sleep later in the morning—calling for the Ithaca secondary schools to have an hour later start time. The Team presented their findings to the School Board [one of the seniors on the team made brownies for the Board to begin the presentation!], and two years later, largely based on these findings [and the fact that the team presented that it would save the District the cost of three fewer school buses], the Superintendent moved the Board to change all the elementary school start times to be 8:00 and the middle and high schools to 9:00. [See other examples of Team Interdisciplinary Graduation Projects in Chapter 2.]

More recently Interdisciplinary Senior Teams have done the following: researched and interviewed 20 community members, and then had a display in the public library about these "unsung local heroes" complete with photos, quotes and short bios; another group surveyed students, teachers, and administrators about their attitudes toward standardized testing, and compared these to the standardized testing practices (or lack of) in Finland schools; and another student planned and carried out an "Infusion Day" on the topic of "Race, Class, and Ethnicity," during which all classes were cancelled for the day, and a series of special workshops were held involving contacting and hosting guest speakers, arranging times and rooms, and creating a schedule for the day.

2. An Individual Senior Project to be presented at the graduation ceremony will:

- Demonstrate the ability to work independently;
- Involve generating ideas, and selecting one, with a specific plan to create an original project;
- Be done outside the expectations of courses and projects;
- Demonstrate a specialized skill or ability or interest;
- Demonstrate life-long learning;

- Involve problem solving, where necessary, including seeking help when and where needed.

Again at the 2017 graduation ceremony there were wonderfully diverse and amazing senior projects, including the following examples—displayed original handmade jewelry, hand-made two dresses one of fabric and one of metal as a sculpture project learned in a vocational welding program, presented a collection of original poetry, performed four original songs accompanied by her father at graduation, formed a music group and performed ten concerts and made an original record, collected toys and clothing for children in the Dominican Republic, made a documentary film about teaching a friend how to juggle, made a short animated cartoon, built a weather station and compared the recordings with a professional one at Cornell University, directed a production of Thornton Wilder's "Our Town," displayed a collection of paintings, and recorded a demo album of original songs on the cello.

3. A LACS Graduation Portfolio which will contain:

- Documentation of "in-depth" study in two or more essential areas;
- An autobiographical sketch;
- Self-reflections on their educational experience;
- A personal resume short-term plans for working and learning;
- A personal plan for maintaining health and physical fitness;
- A projected personal plan/budget for life after graduation;

- Personal recommendations from teachers or those who know the student's work in a variety of areas;
- A collection and analysis of different methodologies of critical thinking and problem-solving;
- Attainment of a level of proficiency for each of the seven essential areas.

Major components of this portfolio are presented to each graduate's Senior Committee, comprised of their Guidance Counselor, Family Group Leader, a parent/caregiver, at least one underclassman, and community member(s) who know the graduate's work. Typically these are great times of celebration, only occasionally requiring a student to complete work in the summer, or even more rarely requiring a student to return in the fall for additional course work.

The Essential Skills, Knowledge, and Attitudes for a Global Citizen

During their school career, students will document their demonstration of proficiency in our core curriculum comprised of the seven Essentials for the Global Citizen (some examples are included below). Our LACS graduates will be:

1. Community Participants and Leaders who:

   - Work and live cooperatively with others;
   - Contribute to the community; and
   - Explore career possibilities.

An example of an activity which addresses the first bullet of this graduation essential, "work and live cooperatively with others," is the annual, two-day Fall Retreat. Quoting from the current Principal's recent newsletter to parents/caregivers about the Fall Retreat: "It is a wonderful tradition—how cool to be in school in the woodsy outdoors! It is one of the important ways we build community. By pushing the 'pause button' on regular classes, we are able to focus on another Essential Area which requires us to practice positive interpersonal skills, cooperate in group decision making, set community goals, accomplish tasks, build community, and engage in self-reflection. Fall Retreat takes a lot of planning, coordinating, and decision-making, and each Family Group is responsible for planning an activity or a game for one of the days. The Retreat is a time to interact with others with whom you might not ordinarily share your day. It is a time to hang out with friends, make new friends, enjoy a game of Survival in the woods, go for long walks, read a book under a tree, play a board game, play some music, and relax."

To fulfill the second bullet, "contribute to the community," students are required to contribute at least 60 hours of community service, at least half of which must be completed outside of LACS in the greater Ithaca community. These have included such things as tutoring elementary school students, assisting with voter registration, volunteering in a local soup kitchen, working with the homeless, or assisting with a physically or mentally challenged adult in one of our senior centers.

And to fulfill the final bullet, "explore career possibilities," a potential graduate must complete at least two of the following: a vocational course at the Tompkins County Board of Cooperative Educational

Services such as childcare or food preparation or auto mechanics, an internship with a one of the professors at Cornell University or Ithaca College as a lab assistant, an internship at a local business establishment such as a law office or the hospital, or an actual work-study part-time paying job at a local business such as a restaurant or retail sales store.

2. Communicators who:

- Read, write, listen, and speak in English;
- Listen, speak, read, and write in a language other than English;[2]
- Use the language of math;[3] and
- Use the personal computer.

3. Critical Thinkers and Problem Solvers who:

- Act on and reflect an anti-bias attitude;[4]
- Use different methods of critical thinking[5] and problem-solving; and
- Use the processes of conflict resolution.

To complete the first bullet of this Essential, students demonstrate that they have taken action to understand and eliminate a bias, reflected on their actions, and reflected on the personal impact of oppression/prejudice/bias. Typically, students will

---

2. This now appears as a separate essential, Communicators in English.
3. This now appears as a separate essential, Problem Solvers who are fluent and reflective in mathematics.
4. This now is included as part of the first essential, Community Participants and Leaders.
5. *Compassionate Critical Thinking: How Mindfulness, Creativity, Empathy and Socratic Questioning Can Transform Teaching,* is a recent book by long time LACS teacher, Ira Rabois.

complete this Essential through coursework, a project, work in the community, or an independent study during their junior and/or senior years. Each student will create a contract with a teacher from the Anti-Bias Team to create an action plan and a plan for reflective analysis. Student reflections will include answering the anti-bias essential questions (What are the historical roots of this bias? What are contemporary examples of this particular bias? How does this/these bias/biases affect you personally?) in a documentable form (writing, video, theater) and engaging in a dialogue with a teacher from the Anti-Bias Team regarding their responses to the questions.

4. Designers, Producers, and Performers who:

    - Pursue concentrated study in one area of the arts—theatre, music, movement, visual arts, media, or technology.

5. Researchers with an Historical and Multicultural Perspective who Understand:

    - U. S. history and the processes of democratic government;
    - Global studies and multiculturalism;
    - Local, national, and global economics.

    For the first bullet above, students will need to demonstrate knowledge and understanding of key concepts and vocabulary in United States history and government (as well as critical thinking skills and a research paper or project) including the following: 1) giving an in-depth explanation of the multiple causes of historical events, including knowledge of social forces such as power and oppression, and how they operate over time; 2) describing the structure and function of the United States government, including knowledge of the historic development of the United States Constitution, legislative processes, and the role of significant Supreme Court decisions; 3) analyzing the roles of people and institutions in struggles for social, economic and political justice and democracy; and 4) describing and analyzing U.S. involvement in global affairs, including the forces that have shaped foreign policy, the impact of U.S. foreign policy, and our concept of democracy.

An example of how the second bullet is partially assessed is the "Middle East Debates," created by one of our social studies teachers. Here students research a historical person currently involved in the middle east conflict, then portray/role play that person in a staging of a United Nations peace conference, which is televised and presented before an invited audience.

6. Contributors to Sustaining the Natural Environment who:

    • Know the key concepts of physical, biological, and chemical components of the environment, and understand their interrelatedness.

    An example of how this essential is partially assessed, developed by one of our science teachers, is a "concept map" that biology students prepare, tracing the path of a food item from the mouth to a region of the body, like a big toe, thus showing the interrelatedness of the human digestive, circulatory, nervous, and muscle systems.

7. Healthy Persons who:

- Demonstrate physical fitness, group participation, and the meeting of personal physical challenges; and
- Demonstrate an understanding of concepts of human sexuality and current major health issues (presently AIDS, and substance use and abuse).[6]

One component of completing the first bullet of this Essential involves taking a physical fitness test, and then, based on the results of that test, designing a personal wellness plan/project. Then, the student (typically in his or her senior year) contracts with a Physical Education teacher to implement a three month plan/project with three stated goals, the means of evaluating if these goals have been met, including personal record keeping and a concluding self-reflection essay.

PBE (Promotion By Exhibition) and GBE (Graduation by Exhibition)[7]

LACS deems students ready for promotion from middle school and graduation from high school once they have completed portfolios and performances that formally demonstrate each student's growth (in middle school) or proficiency (in high school) in each of the outcomes in each of our 10 Essential Areas. While other schools graduate students based on passing classes that earn credit, LACS' outcome-based system requires each student to complete all of their essential demonstrations. At other schools students can "pass a class" with a D and still "earn credit" towards graduation. At LACS each high school student must complete "proficient" (equivalent to a "B" in conventional letter grades) demonstrations in all outcomes in order to graduate. There are no "Cs" or "D's" at LACS.

In our written, narrative evaluation system, teachers identify for each student each cycle if they have Met Expectations or Not Met Expectation for that class (Project, Family Group). Each evaluation will also indicate if a student is On Track or Behind with their portfolio demonstrations. A student may Not Meet Expectations (because of late homework, poor attendance), but still be On Track with their portfolio if they have completed successful demonstrations of essential skills and knowledge. Teacher comments about expectations are intended to help students make progress with their academic Habits so that they can be more successful in school and life. Despite whether or not a student has Met or Not Met expectations, the bottom line for high school graduation is each student's successful portfolio demonstrations in the 10 essential areas. In middle school each student is expected to show growth in their portfolio work to be ready for high school.

While we implemented GBE for the high school component of LACS in the mid-90s, we did not transition the middle school from the old credit system until now. After

6. The list of LACS requirements for high school graduation now includes two additional essentials – #9 "A Scholar who studies in-depth in at least two areas of study or essentials with one or more years beyond the minimum)," and #10 which now simply includes the three initial requirements – "A) a senior interdisciplinary team project, B) an individual senior project, and C) a graduation portfolio."

7. This material is taken from the 2016-17 LACS Footbook and involves modifications made to the original GBE Outcomes and Means of Assessment as well as the middle school/eighth grade "Promotion by Exhibition" in its first experimental year as well as the "OxPort" digital portfolio in its first year of implementation. Both of these changes were developed democratically over more than a year involving input from students and staff.

years of focused work by staff, students and parents/caregivers, we have begun to make the shift to fully implement "PBAT" (Performance Based Assessment Task). Throughout the 2016/17 school year students will begin adding demonstrations to OxPort—the digital portfolio platform, developed over several years by staff working with David Niguidula of Richer Picture and Ideas Consulting Inc.—that show their growth in each of their PBE essential areas. We anticipate that all 8th grade students will be promoted via their OxPort portfolios in the 2018/19 school year.

LACS took a major step forward in fully implementing outcome-based education [as originally called for in the 6th Common Principle of the Coalition of Essential Schools] with the creation of OxPort. In the 2015/16 school year the staff began using OxPort for all evaluations, flags and student goals. During the 2016/17 school year each student entered at least one essential area demonstration (a paper, video, illustration, etc.) and reflection for each class. These were linked to teacher comments and/or evaluation rubrics—indicating that the student had successfully demonstrated progress (in middle school) or proficiency (in high school) in specific essential areas skills and knowledge.

During the 2017/18 school year students in all of the New York Performance Standards Consortium (as mentioned earlier, LACS is a member school) will have to begin to complete the new State Department of Education "Performance–Based Assessment Tasks" (or PBATS). These will involve an analytic literature essay, a social studies research paper, a student-designed science-experiment, and higher-level mathematics problems that have real-world applications. In LACS juniors will experiment with different approaches to the "On Demand" component of the PBATs as follows: in December English will host a "Literary Afternoon" where juniors will present their Literary Analysis PBAT to evaluators and other students; in June the Social Studies Research PBAT will be presented; either in April or in June (along with Social Studies) the Science experiments will be presented; and the Math "Problem Solving" PBAT will be worked on through all the high school upper level classes.

Then, beginning in 2019 for middle school and 2020 for high school, students should have full portfolios in OxPort to show that 8th graders are ready for promotion and 12th graders are ready for graduation. Each student will construct specific "tours" of their OxPort portfolio that will enable colleges, employers or others to view their work. OxPort will enable parents/caregivers, students and staff to easily access student demonstrations, reflections, evaluations and transcripts that will help to focus each student on their strengths, their challenges and the habits needed for success in school and life. While OxPort portfolios will show student demonstrations of essential skills and knowledge, success in school and life is often a reflection of each student's academic and personal habits. Contemporary research has shown that habits of organization, self-awareness, and perseverance are better indicators of success in college, career and life than test scores or grades. In 2014 LACS identified the *Habits* considered the most critical for success (see below). At the beginning of each year each student is asked to assess their strengths and challenges through a *Habits Inventory*. In Family Group, at their mid-year conference and in their evaluations they are asked to reflect on their work towards meeting their goal(s). The staff are committed to teaching these *Habits*[8] throughout our curriculum and to help students to reflect on and grow in their development.

LACS Habits of Responsibility of a Self-Directed Learner:

- Organization such as: come prepared, follow

directions, plan and prioritize your work, break down assignments into doable chunks, keep track of responsibilities, have a time and space to do homework.

- Awareness such as: express anger and frustration appropriately, be aware of anxiousness and how to calm yourself, be open to feedback and be able to make changes, be aware of and appreciate your successes.

- Respect such as: respect others, respect the environment of the school, respect LACS's rules and expectations, use peaceful means to solve conflicts, be open minded to the ideas of others.

- Initiative such as: ask questions, participate, get to school and classes on time, do work without reminders from adults, seek out the help you need, take risks as a learner, speak up for yourself and for others.

- Perseverance such as: stick with something until it is finished, complete work on time, take school attendance seriously, stay focused and pay attention, recognize obstacles and solve problems, be motivated to do your best.

Performance by Exhibition; Middle School Essential Area Requirements

[Note how these basically parallel the high school graduation GBE requirements.]

1. Participants and leaders in the community who:
   a) Work and live cooperatively with others—Full participation in Family Group, School Meetings, Committees, Spring Trips.
   b) Contribute to the community—Community

---

8. These are a recent compilation of the following earlier lists: Habits of Mind and Behavior, Habits of Learning of a Self-Directed Learner, and Habits of Behavior of a Self-Directed Learner.

Service (at least one 9-week cycle of service and one cycle of career explorations).

2. Communicators in English who read, listen, write, speak, present, and think critically: English (10 cycles including 6th grade PAL, "People Art and Literature").

3. Communicators in Global Languages who read, write, listen and speak in a language other than English: Global Languages (begin 3-year high school language sequence typically in Spanish or French which are the main languages available at LACS).

4. Communicators Using Technology who are digitally literate: Computer Literature (two cycles computer literature class or equivalent).

5. Problem Solvers who are fluent and reflective in mathematics: Math (2 or 3-year middle school math sequence before high school math).

6. Designers, Producers And Performers who:
   a) Study the visual arts—Art (three cycles).
   b) Study music and/or theatre arts— Music/Theatre (four cycles).

7. Researchers With A Multicultural Perspective who:
   a) Think critically about US history and government—US History (typically PAL and four cycles of US History).
   b) Think critically about cultures and geography of the world—Global Studies (minimum of two cycles).
   c) Complete an in-depth research project/paper— Research (two cycles, typically in 8th grade).

8. Sustainers of The Environment who study physical and biological science—Science (ten cycles).

9. Healthy Persons who:
   a) Demonstrate physical fitness, group participation

and individual physical skills—PE (eight cycles through classes, PE projects, and/or PE trips).

b) Understand concepts of human sexuality and major health issues—Health (two cycles) .

10. 8th Graders who:

a) Complete their 8th Grade Challenge (an individual project presented at promotion).

Some recent examples of these "Challenge" projects include "Desserts Only Cookbook," "All About North Atlantic Whales," Jazz Dance Project," "Peruvian Folk Music," "French Children's Book," "LACS Snowboard," "Wheelchair Ramp" (for use at the school), "Stop Motion Animation Film," "Original Star Trek Based Episode," Classical Violin Piece," and "Stove for Cooking Made from Tin Cans and Recycled Materials."

Staff Evaluation and Staff Meetings

As the building principal I had the sole responsibility to evaluate the staff. According to the ICSD Teacher's Contract I had to: 1) meet early in the school year with each teacher to select a teaching goal for the year: 2) do a particular number of classroom observations each year with a pre-observation conference and a post-observation conference, then: 3) hold a final evaluation conference; and 4) write out the final evaluation, and 5) have the teacher sign the final evaluation before I submitted it to the Director/Assistant Superintendent of Secondary Education.

For many years I used a blank "goals form" to develop two or three goals with each teacher. Typically these would be things on which a teacher wanted to improve themselves in addition to things we had discussed in the final evaluation of the previous year. These would include such things as—work on having more student-talk time and less teacher-talk time in as many class periods as it makes sense; move about the room more in order to make contact with, if not all, as many students as possible; try something new to more effectively reach some students with whom I am not being fully successful; learn to use the white board effectively; and return work submitted by students in a more timely fashion with meaningful evaluation comments. These would then provide the basis for my classroom observations, often done in a "participant observer" style in which I often became involved with the students, finding out directly what and how they were doing. I would make running notes in a 2-column format on a blank carbon-backed observation form with my notes of what the teacher and students were actually doing throughout the class in one large column with brief comments or questions in the other smaller column, and supportive comments and/or suggestions as I thought of them written in brackets and a kind of italics. At the end of the observation upon leaving the classroom I would tear-off the cover sheet of the observation form, keeping the copy for my own future reference when the post-observation conference was held, usually within a day or two of the observation (I usually scheduled the observation and the post-observation conference when I held the pre-observation conference). This process provided a kind of recording of what I saw and heard during the class from which we could talk about what went well, what might be continued and built upon, and what might need some modification or improvement. I always looked forward to these teacher conferences as we typically had a rich conversation about a given teacher's actual teaching.

When there was a teacher who was struggling and in serious need of improvement, I might schedule more observations with some specific modifications for the given teacher to try. And it was important that these be written down with copies for both of us. Sometimes these would involve a specific "PIP" or "Performance Improvement Plan" with a specific timeline. Rarely did I have to "fire" a teacher. Usually after working through several efforts on my part (and sometimes observations done by another member of our staff support team, a guidance counselor, school social worker, or support teacher) to identify those areas needing serious improvement (as well as those things that were going well). I did not have to officially terminate anyone, they themselves came to the conclusion that teaching—or at least teaching at LACS given all that was expected of them—was not working for them, and they would voluntarily resign. I preferred to work with a teacher over an extended period of time, and not to jump to a conclusion too quickly based solely on a couple of less-than-stellar teaching performances, and I think teachers respected this. Later on, under different district leadership, teachers were "observed" using a very specific detailed "performance observation form" (based on "performance by objectives"). This was a much more formalized process which I tried to find as many ways as possible to circumvent in order to use the above process that we had developed at LACS and that teachers seemed to appreciate and actually found helpful.

Staff meetings (originally held every Wednesday after school for two hours), were often an opportunity for staff to talk with and get help from each other in working with specific students with whom they were struggling. We typically would begin a staff meeting with about a half hour of "staffing" when teachers would identify names of students with whom they were seeking help, and then we would form little clusters of staff to hear what was going on and to offer suggestions, or sometimes do the same but in the whole staff group (often including suggestions from our "Support Team" meetings). From here we would go into the "business" part of the meeting which typically included reviewing what was upcoming in the next few days, or weeks (an All School Meeting, an Infusion Day, parent/caregiver conferences, Spring Trips). Every other Wednesday's Staff meeting was then used for staff "Study Groups" to learn more about something staff were wanting to do in their classes (use of Chrome Books or I-Pads, or White Boards), reading an article or a book together, discussing a proposal before the staff or the whole school which we would work on refining, etc. However, as new staff came on board with a different set of expectations and a more technical adherence to the ICSD Teacher Contract which included fewer staff meetings for less time each month, staff meetings became shorter, not every week, and typically more for business. Here the staff "Agenda Committee," composed of three to five staff members who volunteered each semester or year to facilitate staff meetings, was helpful in making time for the absolute essentials and keeping us on time, although they were excellent facilitators, I felt much was lost in what had originally been a voluntary giving of more meeting time by staff in the early years.

Discussion Questions

1. What would your school view as the essential qualities to be evaluated were you to go to a graduation by exhibition system? What would these be for your eighth graders if you also have a middle school?
2. What would be something special that students could do at your high school graduation and/or middle school promotion?
3. How could you develop the idea that there is no "failure" in your school, only "not yet proficient" or

"has not yet met expectations," with the opportunity to continue working on a particular skill?

4. How are staff evaluated in your school?, and what opportunities are identified for them to work to improve area(s) of deficiency?

Resources

- LACS is one of 27 high schools in New York State to do Graduation by Exhibition, and is a member of the New York Performance Standards Consortium which regards performance assessment as a whole-school based accountability system. To support performance assessment, member schools need to implement seven components, ranging from establishing a culture of active learning to providing multiple ways for students to express and exhibit learning (you can download information about the components at their website: www.performanceassessment.org). Rubrics provide the basis on which to review the quality of student work across four performance tasks: an analytic essay, research paper, science experiment, and applied mathematics (one can download rubric samples). Oversight of the performance assessment system is carried out by an external board—the PAR Board (Performance Assessment Review Board)—which reviews both student work and the process by which it is evaluated. See their publications, student exemplars, sample interim assessments, pacing cards, and forms needed for the high school and middle school at their website.

- The National Center for Fair & Open Testing works to end the misuses and flaws of standardized testing and to ensure that evaluation of students, teachers and schools is fair, open, valid and educationally beneficial. This list includes 990+ institutions that are "test optional," "test flexible" or otherwise de-emphasize the use of standardized tests by making admissions decisions—without using ACT or SAT scores—for all or many applicants who recently graduated from U.S. high schools. They have a number of "Fact Sheets" and other "Resources" on their website, www.fairtest.org.

Afterword

In the spring of 1974, while waiting to hear back from the Ithaca City School District Board of Education if I had been hired as the New Junior High Program teacher/principal, I was playing my guitar on the back steps of the house we'd just temporarily rented, and I wrote a song called "Change Your Ways." It was in the tradition of Bob Dylan's early song-writing, and had a political message. This was/is the third verse:

> "Hey there teacher in your school full of control,
> could it be you've lost sight of your soul?
> Can't you hear the children crying out to be free
> as you grade them A, B, C for their roles?"

It was a critique of education as I'd known it growing up in middle America, in Alexandria, Virginia – essentially teacher-directed, with tracking of students, sorting them into college-bound and non-college-bound, professional and non-professional, winners and losers. In starting NJHP this was a major part of what I wanted to change. It would involve we staff members getting to know our students well, developing genuine caring relationships, helping them find out who they truly were, and what/who they wanted to become.

In the foreword to this book I explained how I came to understand that relationships were the one main or central thing that was most important to me growing up in high school, beginning with my family, my parents, and my older brother. That has stuck with me and I think shows throughout this story of LACS—from Family Groups, Committees, and All School Meetings to Extended Projects, Community Service, Spring Trips and all that's involved in our democratic, shared decision-making. Although the vast majority of our students over those years came from reasonably stable families, there certainly were some who didn't. There were some who dropped-out, a few who were incarcerated, and a small handful who took their own lives. Yet many of our most troubled students made it, largely because there was a significant adult who cared deeply about them—sometimes a grandmother, a single mother, a minister or rabbi, even a neighbor, and more often than not, one of our staff members. And all that was about relationships!

Returning then to *A Principal's Notebook*, there were many pages filled over the years with notes from meetings with families, parents/caregivers, community people, trying to figure out a particular student and how to help him or her to stay in school, to make it, and in some way to become successful. Often, while taking notes in that notebook at school district meetings or education conferences, I would be thinking of one or more of our students about whom I was particularly concerned at the time, and I would insert parenthetically, in italics, notes about an idea that had just come to me—how I might do something to help, or someone to contact who might be able to help. Thus, as I close this last chapter of the Story of the Lehman Alternative Community School, and close *The Notebook*, it is not the end of the story. LACS continues serving the families of Ithaca, New York. So to all of you currently at LACS, and to all of you reading this story; my story, of one, public, alternative, secondary school that still tries to keep relationships at the center, at the heart of all they do—godspeed!

Appendix

From the beginning of the New Junior High Program until the present Lehman Alternative Community School, there has been a commitment to govern the school democratically. Thus, as Principal, I was involved from the beginning to work nationally and at the state level to create organizations to spread this idea of democratic education. In May of 1976, some NJHP staff and myself attended the "Education for Change" international conference at DePaul University in Chicago, Illinois where we formed the "National Coalition of Alternative Community Schools" (NCACS), and I co-authored the following statement of purpose:

> We are a national coalition of schools, groups, and individuals committed to creating an egalitarian society by working against racism, sexism, ageism and all forms of social, political, and economic oppression. We support an educational process which is alternative in:
>
> 1. Intention—we work to empower people to actively and collectively direct their lives;
> 2. Form—we support the active control of education by students, parents, teachers, and other community members;

3. Content—we develop the tools and skills to effect social change.

The National Coalition brings together and supports all schools, or groups, or individuals which work toward these ends."

Subsequently, working with other alternative educators over the years we created the "New York State Coalition of Educational Alternatives" (NYSAEA), the "Ohio Coalition of Educational Alternatives Now" (OCEAN, "we make big waves!"), as well as "New York Performance Standards Consortium," and similar organizations from California and Montana to Indiana and Michigan (there now are such organizations in 37 of the 48 states!).

At one point in the development of LACS, one of our students took a proposal to the All School Meeting to create a constitution since we were a democratic institution. This was approved by the school community and he subsequently chaired a student committee to draft such a document, and in the process our students of color pointed out that they were left out of the U.S. Constitution. Thus it became the "Decision-Making Document." The current 2010 revision of this important document is attached. I would point out that the Principal—although part of the ASM and staff meetings—essentially has only two sole responsibilities (in addition to the school district's requirement to supervise and evaluate staff): 1) confidential issues of punishment (those discipline issues which cannot come before the Alternative Community Court—now the Restorative Justice Council—e.g. school suspensions, although the Court can recommend suspension), and 2) the immediate health and safety of all people in the school (e.g. evacuation of the building in an emergency).

Shared Decision-Making Document

Preamble: We, the members of the Lehman Alternative Community School [a cover page to the document was actually signed by all the students and staff present at the ASM where it was approved!], being of sound mind and body, wishing to bring our school out of the murky, primordial waters of our democratic past, and desiring the purity, cleanliness, and clarity of order, desire adoption of the following system of site-based self-government. May order prevail unto eternity.

Purpose: The purpose of the Decision-Making Document (DMD) is to lay out guidelines for the LACS community which clearly define who gets to decide what in our school. The Decision-Making Document is to be used by the school and community to demonstrate where a new proposal goes and general guidelines defining how that proposal shall be decided. While this purpose shall remain the basis for the document, we realize that the document itself shall need revision as the school matures. A process for amending this document is included in Section-F in the Appendix.

History: This Decision-Making Document arose from the uncertainty Agenda Committee faced in the mid-1990s. A proposal was brought to the Committee, and Agenda was unable to decide if it should be brought before the students in All School Meetings or before staff in staff meeting. The question of who should decide this proposal led to the creation of a student "Constitution Committee," which was to draft guidelines for the school that would decide what sorts of proposals would come to staff, what would go to students, and what would be decided by other groups. Agenda would then use this document, upon approval by the school, to decide where the controversial proposal—or others like it—would go. This document is the combination of student and staff versions, with parent/caregiver input through the LACS site-based council.

In 2008-9, the school community began to feel a lack of ownership over the school democracy. Many felt that the layers of bureaucracy were interfering with the ability for involvement with the governance of the school. To address these issues, a group of students proposed a committee be formed to examine the school democracy and create a proposal to change the democratic systems. The "Reconstitution Committee" first met second semester 2008-09, and after a year of examining the school's feedback, brought a proposal in early 2010, which simplified the previous system answering the question: How is school government at LACS organized? What school groups can make decisions about what?

A) LACS Council/Site Based Council (SBC)

Many of the members of the Site Based Council (SBC) are staff and students, and thus are already represented in other decision-making processes. Although the Council is accorded specific responsibilities, its main responsibilities should be to review and advise.

1. Non-decision making responsibilities
    a) Council must gather input from all concerned parties before making decisions.
    b) Council must publicly post its decisions, both in full and in a quick, easy to read format (perhaps on posters).
2. Decision Making Responsibilities
    a) Deciding how decisions are made in the SBC.
    b) Final say on interpretation of this document if agreement cannot be reached on the correct interpretation: (1) Creating a proposal to clarify or amend this document once decided.

c) Creating and implementing admissions policy (to be shared with the school).

d) Recommendations to Principal concerning: (1) Budget (2) Hiring/dismissal of Staff (3) Buildings and grounds.

e) Specific goals (to be shared with school): (1) Five-Year School Development Plan (2) Other concrete goals.

f) Allocation of Special Funds.

B) Staff Meetings

A staff-only group that decides when and which classes and projects are offered and may check proposals voted on in ASM in some circumstances (see appendix A)

1. Non-Decision Making Responsibilities

a) Posting all decisions made by Staff Meeting that fall under this document. These decisions must be posted in a public location, both in full and in a quick, easy to read fashion.

b) Getting student input and being receptive to student input for all matters relating to when and what classes, projects, family group, etc. are offered. To be achieved by evaluations of classes, informal questionnaires, petitions, or other methods that may arise.

c) Making sure that there are enough courses to fulfill all Middle School Challenges and High School Graduation Requirements.

d) Notifying students of expectations for each individual class/project/committee.

2. Decision Making Responsibilities

a) When classes and projects are offered, excluding student led classes or projects.

b) Who teaches what classes and projects, excluding student led classes or projects.

c) Requirements and expectations of individual classes, projects, committees.

d) Check of ASM decisions (See appendix A).

e) Deciding how decisions are made in Staff Meetings.

C) All-School Meetings (ASM)

LACS's version of direct democracy: one person, one vote. Staff and students both involved for all decisions.

1. Non-Decision Making Responsibilities
Posting all decisions made in a public location, both in full and in a quick, easy to read fashion.

2. Decision Making Responsibilities

a) Creation and Destruction of Committees. (1) Committees may serve new needs or assist in responsibilities originally accorded to ASM. (2) ASM may vote to suspend/destroy a committee that no longer serves the school's needs.

b) Deciding how decisions are made in School Meetings.

c) Fall Retreat: (1) When it occurs, and (2) All other matters unless interfering with district policy.

d) Rights and responsibilities: (1) Expectations and agreements of behavior, (2) Processes for dealing with violation(s) of expectations.

e) School Look: (1) Flags/Logos/Etc.

f) Spring Trips: (1) Date they occur, (2) Allocation of funds.

g) Philosophy Statements (see glossary).

h) Timetable: (1) How the day is broken into periods (see appendix C), (2) How the week is divided, i.e.; when morning meeting, family group, etc. happen, (3) Whole school events during the school day.

i) Amending this document.

j) Graduation Requirements; creating and modifying: (1) GBE Essentials, (2) Middle School Challenges; (3) Any other graduation requirements.

k) Formal evaluations of students, staff, and teaching: (1) How such evaluation takes place, (2) Appearance of forms, (3) Content of forms.

l) Modifying rationales for Staff Check.

m) LACS attendance policy.

D) Students as a Group

1. Election of Representatives to:
   a) Site Based Council
   b) School Board

E) Committees

Committees are an integral part of School decision-making. However, the continually evolving nature of committees would make it difficult to include a list of the responsibilities of each committee in this document. A committee creates its own goals and responsibilities as long as they do not conflict or vary drastically from the original goals agreed upon when the committee was created. A list of current committees should be included with this document for reference only.

1. Non decision making responsibilities
    a) Posting all decisions made that significantly affect the day to day operation of the school in a public location (examples of committees that should always do this include the student court (Restorative Justice Council), the committee that works on rights and responsibilities).
2. Changing purpose of committees
    a) A committee may not significantly change its purpose or goals without resubmitting to All School Meeting. This should not be an issue, because in most cases a new committee could be formed achieving the same end.
3. Forming committees
    a) Committees must be approved by All School Meeting. Once a committee has been approved, a staff member must be found to lead or supervise the committee.

F. The Principal

The Principal is part of ASM and staff meeting, but has a few additional powers which are mandated by the school board and the LACS decision-making structure.

1. Non-Decision Making Powers
    a) Posting and/or announcing all decisions made in a public manner.
    b) Supervise and evaluate staff.
2. Decision-Making Powers
    a) Confidential issues of punishment: (1) Discipline issues which cannot come before the Alternative Community Court; ACC should be notified and should review the

decision without names being included in the case.

b) Immediate health and safety issues: (1) Note: any issue which must be decided on before it could be resolved through an ASM, (2) A vote of confidence should be taken by ASM about the decision—i) At this time, the students may propose alternative resolutions; ii) This vote is non-binding, but should be taken into consideration by the Principal.

Shared Decision-Making Document Appendix and Notes

A. Staff Check Process—The "Staff Check Process" is a process to ensure that no decisions are made by ASM that will significantly harm the school community.

1. All proposals passed by ASM, except those which fall under the purview of "how decisions are made in ASM" and initiating vote of the "automatic review" process (see Appendix J), are subject to review and possible check by the staff.

2. Staff do not have to review every proposal voted on; instead, the staff check process will be initiated by a staff member if they feel that a decision made by ASM will significantly harm the school community

3. Staff wishing to review a decision must announce/post publicly that they are doing so within 10 school days and also notify Agenda Committee.

4. Staff meeting must then review the proposal within three full staff meetings from the time of the announcement to the school. Once they are done reviewing, they must post and/or announce

their decision and a rationale for their decision publicly.

5. The proposal may be re-written (by the author or another interested party) in order to address the rationale brought up by the staff. The revised proposal will then be brought back to an ASM.

6. Staff check requires staff consensus that the proposal passed by ASM will significantly harm the school community.

7. The staff may only check a proposal if it: a) Would be a hazard to the health of any student or staff member; b) Would break staff contracts; c) Would go against the philosophy statements of the school ; d) Would change a staff power listed in the document; e) Would be harmful to teaching; f) Would cause an undue loss of teaching time; g) Would cause a loss of teaching time to an event that was not properly planned.

8. The staff may propose new rationales for the staff check process, but these rationales must be approved by ASM.

B. Submitting Proposals

1. To a group that you are a member of:

a) Each decision making group (for example, Staff Meeting, School Meetings) will establish its own guidelines on submission of proposals. However, any person must be allowed to make a proposal, pursuant to guidelines established in this document and any guidelines the group itself may make from time to time.

b) These guidelines must be clearly and publicly posted.

2. If you are a parent/caregiver or community member, including alumni:
   a) You may submit a proposal to any school decision-making group.
   b) You must find a "sponsor" to bring that proposal to the correct group. You have the right to participate in that decision making group's process but may not vote. That sponsor must be a member of the school, but not necessarily the group that will decide on the proposal.
3. To a group of which you are not a member:
   a) Any group or individual may submit a proposal to be reviewed by any decision making group. That proposal will then be decided by that group using their regular process. You have the right to participate in that process but may not vote.

C. Timetable

1. If any person wishes to make a change for the next school year which would affect the timetable (for example, offering all double-period classes) or change the timetable directly that person must bring his or her idea to All School Meeting in the year before the change would go into effect, no matter what group would normally make that decision. This does not prevent staff from scheduling individual classes over the summer.

D. Consistency with Goals

1. Any person who feels that a decision was made that was inconsistent with school goals or philosophy should bring a proposal to change that decision to the appropriate group.

a) A person outside of the regular decision making body should contact that decision-making body with their concerns, who will then determine the appropriate handling of the problem.

2. Agenda should confer with the author and schedule that proposal for the very next regular school meeting, or recommend that an Emergency All School Meeting be called (see Appendix section I).

E) If this Document is Incorrectly Interpreted:

A change is made by a group or process which should not have had purview over it, or a process is misused.

1. The person who notices makes an appeal to Agenda Committee.

2. Agenda compares the issue to the outline of purview described "What School Groups Can Make Decisions About What?"

3. If the outline of purview is clear on the correct process and only a simple mistake was made:

a) The decision is suspended.

b) Agenda notifies the school body of the problem.

c) Agenda sends the proposal through the correct process to be decided again.

4. If the outline of purview is unclear on the correct process

a) The proposal is reviewed by Site Based Council.

(1) If Site Based Council thinks it was decided using the correct process.

(a) The decision is allowed to stand.

(2) If Site Based Council thinks it was decided under the wrong process.
   (a) The decision is suspended.
   (b) Site Based Council notifies the school.
   (c) The proposal is brought through the correct process as determined by SBC.

b) No matter how Site Based Council decides, Site Based Council creates a proposal to amend this document, to prevent future confusion.

c) That proposal is sent through the usual process for amending this document.

F) Amendments to this document

1. If a person wishes to amend this document, he or she will write a proposal proposing his or her amendment.

a) That proposal is brought to ASM.

b) The proposal alone is voted on, not this document. If the proposal is enacted, this document is changed to reflect that amendment. This document as a whole will not need to be re-ratified.

c) An updated copy of this document should be kept by Agenda and should be made publicly available to any person.

2. A change of name to this document is considered an amendment to the document, and should therefore follow the process of amending the document.

3. If the name of a group mentioned in this document is changed.

a) The name change is sent to Site Based Council.

> b) Site Based Council decides whether to update this document to reflect the name change. The update does not need to go through the entire process of amending this document.

4. Lists and other descriptors, including the "current voting practices" list and the list of current committees, may be updated by the group that maintains this document without amending this document.

G) Current Voting Practices

These are useful only as guides as to how things are now. They should not be construed as actual guidelines, as each group can decide on their own voting practices without amending this document. This list should be updated on any change.

1. Site Based Council currently votes by consensus.
2. Staff Meeting currently votes by consensus.
3. School Meeting currently votes by a 2/3 majority of combined student/staff votes.
4. Notes:

> a) "Consensus" currently means that all who vote can live with a decision, not that all are necessarily for it.

> b) "2/3 majority" means that 2/3 or more of those voting (excluding abstentions) are in favor of a proposal. The rationale of excluding abstentions is that, if they were to be included, they would in effect count as "no" votes by raising the number of votes needed to reach a 2/3 majority.

H) Posting of Decisions

Groups that are required to post the decisions that they make should post all such decisions in one shared central location. This includes School Meeting proposals, Staff Meeting proposals, Site Based Council minutes, and committees that make decisions (such as the Student Court). It might be a good idea to include other minutes on this "wall of democracy" (such as ICSD School Board Meeting minutes).

I. Calling an Emergency ASM (EASM)

An emergency ASM can be called in different ways. The purpose of an EASM is to allow for issues that need to be dealt with immediately to come to ASM in a timely fashion.

1. How to call an EASM

a) The principal may call an EASM at any time

b) Any student or staff member may call an EASM by writing a petition which specifies the topic to be dealt with and the time that the EASM will occur.

(1) A petition to create a new ASM time must be signed by 50 students and 15 staff

(2) To supersede a previously scheduled ASM agenda the petition must be signed by any 65 community members.

2. This meeting will be run in the manner specified by the petition or principal

3. Agenda Committee will supply a leader/co-leader as requested by the proposal.

J. Automatic Review

1. Every four years Agenda Committee will call an

ASM to review our democratic process. In this ASM, the entire school will vote on any questions about the school's democracy and whether it needs change. Automatic Review cannot be checked by the staff.

2. This process may be initiated at any time if a proposal is brought to do so. The process will automatically be started again four years after it has last been brought to an ASM.

CPSIA information can be obtained
at www.ICGtesting.com
Printed in the USA
BVHW03s1234110618
518747BV00025B/1626/P

9 780986 016028